JOHN WESLEY'S
EXTRACT OF

The

Rule

and

Exercises

of

Holy

Living

AND

Dying

JOHN WESLEY'S
EXTRACT OF

The Rule and Exercises of Holy Living AND Dying

BY JEREMY TAYLOR

The John Wesley Collection
Andrew C. Thompson
Executive Editor

 Seedbed

Scripture quotations throughout are the author's paraphrase.

Printed in the United States of America

Cover design by Strange Last Name
Page design and layout by PerfecType, Nashville, Tennessee

Taylor, Jeremy, 1613-1667.
John Wesley's extract of The rule and exercises of holy living and holy dying / by Jeremy Taylor. – Frankin, Tennessee : Seedbed Publishing, ©2018.

pages ; cm. – (John Wesley collection)

Previously published as: The rule and exercises of holy living, and, The rule and exercises of holy dying / by Jeremy Taylor ; edited and abridged by John Wesley in his A Christian library : consisting of extracts from and abridgments of the choicest pieces of practical divinity. Volume 9. Bristol, England : printed by Felix Farley, 1749-1755.
.
ISBN 9781628242904 (paperback)
ISBN 9781628242911 (Mobi)
ISBN 9781628242928 (ePub)
ISBN 9781628242935 (uPDF)

1. Christian life--Anglican authors--Early works to 1800. 2. Death--Religious aspects--Christianity--Early works to 1800. I. Title. II. Rule and exercises of holy living and holy dying. III. Rule and exercises of holy living. IV. Rule and exercises of holy dying. V. Wesley, John, 1703-1791,

BV4500.T28 2018   248.4/83   2018955273

 Seedbed

SEEDBED PUBLISHING
Franklin, Tennessee
seedbed.com

CONTENTS

Publisher's Foreword   vii

Introduction   ix

PART I: THE RULE AND EXERCISES
OF HOLY LIVING

I. Of the General Instruments and Means
   Serving to a Holy Life   3

II. Of Christian Sobriety   19

III. Of Christian Justice   47

PART II: THE RULE AND EXERCISES
OF HOLY DYING

I. A General Preparation toward a Holy and
   Blessed Death, by Way of Consideration   63

II. A General Preparation toward a Holy and
    Blessed Death, by Way of Exercise   83

III. Of the State of Sickness, and the Temptations
     Incident to It, with Their Proper Remedies   91

IV. Of the Practice of the Graces Proper to the
    State of Sickenss   101

V. Of Visitation of the Sick   109

PUBLISHER'S FOREWORD

John Wesley's profound legacy and impact on world Christianity in his lifetime and since can be viewed through several lenses. The revival that arose under his leadership changed the social and political structure of eighteenth-century England as the poor and lost found hope in the gospel of Jesus Christ rather than in revolution against the crown. The influence of Wesley's Spirit-inspired teaching continued unabated as the Methodist movement spread scriptural holiness across the American continent and lands far beyond.

Wesley's influence as a publisher represents an astonishing record in its own right. Wesley lived in a time when Gutenberg's invention of movable type, which had immediately preceded Luther's Reformation, had coalesced into specialized printing trades in London. Typefounders and printeries offered exciting new pathways for the spread of the gospel through inexpensive printed text.

Perhaps more than any other figure of his day, Wesley embraced this new technology and issued sermons, tracts, commentaries, abridgments, biographies, and a host of other items that he considered relevant to the spiritual growth of maturing Christians.

Wesley was vitally driven by the reality of the inner witness of the Holy Spirit. His teaching on entire sanctification, or Christian perfection, is the capstone of his legacy. He worked tirelessly to abridge and republish seminal works by historical figures of previous generations, reaching as far back as the apostolic fathers of the first-century church. He constantly curated voices that communicated the work of the Holy Spirit in bringing believers into the fullness of salvation and lives of holy love.

These writings resourced the early Methodists in their quest to spread the gospel by providing the intellectual and spiritual moorings for the messengers of the movement. Seedbed believes these writings are as relevant today as they were in the eighteenth and nineteenth centuries.

With great joy we present The John Wesley Collection. In the years ahead, Seedbed will reissue selections from this vast collection, which includes his fifty-volume Christian Library, some 150 sermons, countless items from his journals and letters, as well as innumerable tracts, hymns, poems, and other publications, most of which have been out of circulation for decades, if not centuries. We encourage you to enter these texts with determination. Readers who persevere will soon find themselves accustomed to the winsome tenor and tempo of Wesley's voice and vernacular.

Seedbed's editors are constantly examining the more than 250 years of vital spiritual writing by Wesley and successive generations to find the most relevant and helpful messages that will speak to today's body of believers. We commend this old-new publishing work to you as one ready to be transformed by the latent power of these ancient truths. It is our prayer that these timeless words will add fuel to the fire of an awakening ready to ignite once again across the world.

Sola sancta caritas! Amen.

Andrew Miller
Seedbed Publishing

INTRODUCTION

Bishop Jeremy Taylor was one of the early influences on John Wesley's understanding of holy living. Wesley mentions the impact that reading Taylor had on him as a young man at Oxford University in the opening paragraphs of *A Plain Account of Christian Perfection*. Taylor's meditations on holy living and holy dying left Wesley "exceedingly affected," especially in the seventeenth-century bishop's view on the purity of intention. In response to reading Taylor, Wesley reports that he "resolved to dedicate all my life to God." He became convinced that there could be no middle ground between serving God and living a worldly life. Wesley says that there could be "no medium, but that every part of my life . . . must either be a sacrifice to God, or myself; that is, in effect, to the devil."[1] The mid-1720s marked the beginning of the spiritual journey that would carry John Wesley to the leadership of the Methodist revival in subsequent years. In that sense, the impact of Taylor and other writers of the holy living tradition on Wesley's life was pivotal.

The Life of Jeremy Taylor

Jeremy Taylor's adult life was lived during one of the most tumultuous periods in English history. Taylor was born in the year 1613 and came of age during the early years of the reign of King Charles I (1625–1649). He did not come from a wealthy

---

1. John Wesley, *A Plain Account of Christian Perfection*, ¶2 (Peterborough, UK: Epworth Press, 1952), 5.

family; though he obtained a first-rate education at Gonville and Caius College, Cambridge, Taylor was only able to attend through a scholarship. He matriculated at the university in 1629 with the status of a *pauper scholaris*.[2]

Taylor was ordained to the priesthood of the Church of England in 1633 and soon caught the attention of William Laud, the new archbishop of Canterbury. Taylor's theological and ecclesiastical leanings were shared by Laud. With the young priest's high churchmanship and devotion to patristic theology, the archbishop likely saw a potential protégé whom he could develop and use in his efforts to reform the Church of England in an increasingly High Church direction. Thus, Taylor gained preferment under Laud's influence. He first received a fellowship at All Souls' College, Oxford, and subsequently was made chaplain to the archbishop. In 1638, he was appointed as rector of Uppingham parish in the diocese of London.[3] As Taylor's career began to take off, he married a woman named Phoebe Langsdale and started a family with her that would produce numerous children.

Time was not on Taylor's side with respect to political developments in England, however. The personal rule of Charles I without parliament proved to be deeply unpopular, and Charles's chief ministers such as Laud and Thomas Wentworth, Earl of Strafford, would bear much of the Long Parliament's anger once it was called into session in the fall of 1640. Wentworth was attainted and beheaded in May of 1641. Laud suffered the same fate in January of 1645.[4] England was thrown into civil war between those loyal to the king and those loyal to parliament

---

2. Thomas K. Carroll, ed., *Jeremy Taylor: Selected Works* (Mahwah, NJ: Paulist Press, 1990), 16.

3. Ibid., 17–18.

4. Robert Bucholz and Newton Key, *Early Modern England, 1485–1714: A Narrative History* (Malden, MA: Wiley-Blackwell, 2009), 244–47.

in the late summer of 1642. As the Parliamentarians (with their Puritan religious tendencies) gained the upper hand over time, the clergy who were associated with Laud were made to suffer. Taylor was forced to leave his parish appointment at Uppingham and, like many of his countrymen, lived an uncertain existence over the next several years.[5]

Jeremy Taylor wrote his twin works on holy living and holy dying during a difficult time in England generally and in his life in particular. He lived under the protection of the Earl and Countess of Carbery at their Golden Grove estate during the later stages of the civil war and the beginning of the interregnum. Yet it was not a happy time for him.[6] King Charles was executed by order of parliament in 1649; his patron Frances Vaughan, the countess of Carbery, died in 1650; and Taylor's first wife, Phoebe, died in 1651. In the midst of both national and personal loss, Taylor wrote *The Rule and Exercises of Holy Living* in 1650 and *The Rule and Exercises of Holy Dying* in 1651. The two works "soon became one ... in popular piety" and are to this day often referred to as simply *The Rule and Exercises of Holy Living and Dying*.[7]

Eventually the political tenor of England changed. Charles I's son was invited back to England from the Netherlands in 1660 to take the throne as Charles II, and the restoration of the monarchy brought with it a restoration of the Church of England. Taylor was made bishop over the minor diocese of Down and Connor in Ireland—certainly not the type of reward for which the faithful royalist pastor might have hoped, but at least a small vindication for what he and his family had suffered over the previous years. Unfortunately, the diocese's predominantly Presbyterian-leaning population cared nothing for episcopal oversight, and the years that the now-Bishop Taylor spent overseeing it were not happy ones.

---

5. Carroll, ed., 20–21.

6. Ibid., 22–27.

7. Ibid., 433.

He died in 1667, having buried a wife and seven sons who predeceased him.[8] Taylor led a difficult life in a difficult time, yet he still managed to produce some of the most significant theological works of the seventeenth-century English church. Of those works, *Holy Living* and *Holy Dying* stand as among the most important meditations on Christian piety that have been written in English since the Reformation.

The Influence of *Holy Living* and *Holy Dying* on John Wesley

Taylor's writing style is accessible enough, even if the holy living genre in which he writes is presently out of fashion. It's true that, at times, Taylor can veer into a kind of moralism that seems pedantic and overdone. But his writing also has the ability to rise to the level of the sublime. He sees the presence of God in all the works of creation, and encourages his reader to do the same:

> In the face of the sun you may see God's beauty; in the fire you may feel his heat warming; in the water his gentleness to refresh you. He it is who comforts your spirits when you have taken cordials. It is the dew of heaven that makes your field give you bread; and the breasts of God are the bottles that minister drink to your necessities.

It is this deep and profound sense that we live in the presence of God at every moment that serves as the basis for Taylor's views on holy living. We are the creatures of a Holy God—even more, we are the image bearers of that God. Thus are we called to live our lives in moment-by-moment response to the God who has created us and who redeems us, according to Taylor's counsel: "Let us remember that God is in us, and that we are in

---

8. Carroll, ed., 33–37.

him. We are his workmanship, let us not deface it; we are in his presence, let us not pollute it by unholy actions."

The impact of Jeremy Taylor on Wesley was significant. As the historian Richard Heitzenrater has shown, the holy living tradition as represented by Taylor and others (e.g., Thomas à Kempis) had both outward and inward influences on Wesley's spirituality. Taylor's writings on holy living in particular caused Wesley to see that holiness should embrace the way in which he spent the hours and minutes of every day. To that end, he began to keep a diary to serve as a daily record of how he spent his time and how he was making progress in holiness. It was also through the holy living writers that Wesley came to understand holiness itself as an inward reality—a disposition of the heart that would guide one's thoughts, words, and actions. The meditative and reflective nature of Taylor's writings certainly served as an impetus to this developing aspect of Wesley's theological perspective.[9]

Wesley understood the lived context of the Christian life to be built upon the believer's use of the means of grace—those practices either instituted by Christ or recommended by prudence that bring us into contact with God's sanctifying grace. Thus, we can find many instances of Wesley speaking about the instituted or prudential means of grace as the vehicles for spiritual growth and maturation. There is also a third category of the means of grace in Wesley's understanding, however, which is often overlooked because it is not as clearly delineated in Wesley's writings on the means of grace. This category is the general means of grace, and Wesley employs it at those places where he wants to speak to the importance of the intention of

---

9. Richard P. Heitzenrater, *Wesley and the People Called Methodists*, second edition (Nashville, TN: Abingdon Press, 2013), 39–41. A fuller treatment of this theme can be found in Heitzenrater's chapter, "The Meditative Piety of the Oxford Methodists," in Richard P. Heitzenrater, *Mirror and Memory: Reflections on Early Methodism* (Nashville, TN: Kingswood Books, 1989), 78–105.

our hearts and minds when we use any of the means of grace.[10] One of the phrases he employs to talk about the use of the general means of grace is "the exercise of the presence of God." It's a phrase that points to his belief that we are never truly apart from God and, indeed, always have the ability to reach out to God through faith. He uses it in the 1784 sermon, "On Dissipation," and perhaps not surprisingly, it comes in a paragraph following a citation of Jeremy Taylor's view on the purity of intention in the *The Rule and Exercises of Holy Living*.[11] The general means of grace serve as the foundation for the life of sanctification for Wesley, and Taylor's account of holiness was a significant influence on the development of that understanding.

The Edition Used in This Volume

Wesley sought to make both the *The Rule and Exercises of Holy Living* and *The Rule and Exercises of Holy Dying* more widely available to the English reading public through his inclusion of Jeremy Taylor in his multivolume Christian Library. The Christian Library was Wesley's most ambitious publishing project, encompassing fifty volumes of theological writings that he brought to print between 1749 and 1755. Volume 16 of the Christian Library (published in 1752) contained Wesley's abridgment of both *Holy Living* and *Holy Dying*.[12]

---

10. See Andrew C. Thompson, "The General Means of Grace," *Methodist History* 51:4 (July 2013): 249–57.

11. John Wesley, "On Dissipation," ¶¶18–19, in vol. 3 of *The Bicentennial Edition of the Works of John Wesley*, ed. Albert C. Outler (Nashville, TN: Abingdon Press, 1986), 123.

12. See Richard P. Heitzenrater, "John Wesley's A Christian Library, Then and Now," *American Theological Library Association Summary of Proceedings* 55 (2001): 137. I am also most grateful to Dr. Randy L. Maddox of Duke University for additional information about the volume contents of the Christian Library.

While the Christian Library went through just one edition in Wesley's lifetime, it was republished between 1819 and 1827 by Thomas Jackson. This edition contained the breadth of Wesley's original material in only thirty volumes, and Jeremy Taylor's writings were placed in Volume 9. The Wesley Center Online at Northwest Nazarene University in Nampa, Idaho, has produced a digital edition of the nineteenth-century Jackson edition of the Christian Library, and the abridgment of Taylor in this present volume has been drawn from that text.[13]

Andrew C. Thompson, ThD
Executive Editor

---

13. The website for the Wesley Center Online at Northwest Nazarene University can be found at http://wesley.nnu.edu/.

PART I

The Rule
and Exercises
of Holy Living

I.

OF THE GENERAL INSTRUMENTS
AND MEANS SERVING TO
A HOLY LIFE

Introduction

It is necessary that every man should consider that since God has given him an excellent nature, an understanding soul, and an immortal spirit, having made him lord over the beasts, and but a little lower than the angels; he has appointed for him a work and a service great enough to employ those abilities, and has designed him to a state of life after this, to which he can only arrive by that service and obedience. Therefore, as every man is wholly God's own portion by the title of creation, so all our labor and care, all our powers and faculties, must be wholly employed in the service of God, even all the days of our life; that this life being ended, we may live with him forever. Neither is it sufficient that we think of the service of God as a work of small employment, but that it be done by us as God intended it; that it be done with great earnestness and passion, with much zeal and desire; that we refuse no labor, that we bestow upon it much time, that we use the best guides, and arrive at the end of glory by all the ways of grace, of prudence, and religion.

And, indeed, if we consider how much of our lives is taken up by the needs of nature, how many years are wholly spent before we come to any use of reason, how many years more before that reason be useful to us to any great purposes; how imperfect our discourse is made by our evil education, false principles, ill company, bad examples, and lack of experience; how many parts of our best years are wholly spent in eating and sleeping, in necessary businesses and unnecessary vanities; in learning arts and sciences, languages or trades; that little portion of hours that is left for the practice of piety and walking with God is so short, that were not the goodness of God infinitely great, it might seem unreasonable to expect of him eternal joys in heaven, even after spending well those few minutes which are left for God and God's service. And yet the fruit that comes from the many days of vanity is very little. But from the few hours we spend in prayer and the exercises of a pious life, the return is great and profitable; and what we sow in the minutes of a few years grows up to crowns and scepters in a glorious eternity.

1. Therefore, although it cannot be enjoined that the greatest part of our time should be spent in the direct actions of devotion, yet it is not only a duty, but also a great providence, to lay aside for the services of God and the businesses of the Spirit as much as we can. Because God rewards our minutes with eternal happiness; and the greater portion of our time we give to God, the more we treasure up for ourselves. No man is a better merchant than he who lays out his time upon God, and his money upon the poor.

2. It becomes us to remember and adore God's goodness, for God has not only permitted us to serve the necessities of our nature, but has made them parts of our duty; that if we, by directing these actions to the glory of God, intend them as instruments to continue our persons in his service, he, by adopting them into religion, may turn our nature into grace, and accept our natural actions as actions of religion. God is pleased to esteem it a part of his service for us to eat or drink, so it be done temperately, and as may best preserve our health; that our

health may enable us to perform our services toward him. And there is not one minute of our lives (after we have come to the use of reason), but we are and may be doing the work of God, even then when we most of all serve ourselves.

3. To which if we add, that in these and all other actions of our lives, we always stand before God, acting, and speaking, and thinking in his presence; and that it matters not that we have our conscience sealed with secrecy, since it lies open to God; it will concern us to behave ourselves carefully, as in the presence of our Judge.

These three considerations, applied to the several parts and instances of our lives, will be, like Elisha stretched upon the child, apt to put life and quickness into every part of it, and to make us live the life of grace, and do the work of God. I shall therefore, by way of introduction, reduce them to practice, and show how every Christian may improve all and each of them to the advantage of piety, in the whole course of his life.

Section I

The First General Instrument of Holy Living: Care of Our Time

He who is choice of his time will also be choice of his company, and choice of his actions; lest the first engage him in vanity and loss, and the latter, by being criminal, be a throwing of his time and himself away, and a going back in the accounts of eternity. God has given to man a short time upon earth, and yet upon this short time eternity depends; so that for every hour of our life (after we know good from evil), we must give an account to the great Judge of men and angels.

For we must remember that we have a great work to do: many enemies to conquer, many evils to prevent, much danger to run through, many difficulties to be mastered, many necessities to serve, and much good to do; many children to provide for, or many friends to support, or many poor to relieve, or many diseases to cure; besides our private and our public cares, and duties of the world, which the providence of God has adopted into the family of religion.

The life of every man may (and, indeed, must) be so ordered that it may be a perpetual serving of God. The greatest trouble and most busy trade, when they are necessary, or charitable, or profitable, in order to any of those ends which we are bound to serve, whether public or private, being a doing of God's work. For God provides the good things of the world to serve the needs of nature, by the labors of the ploughman, the skill and pains of the artisan, and the dangers and traffic of the merchant; these men are in their callings the ministers of the divine providence, and the stewards of the creation, and servants of a great family of God, the world, in procuring necessaries for food and clothing, ornament and physic. In their proportions also, a king, a priest, a prophet, a judge, and an advocate, doing the work of their employment according to their proper rules, are doing the work of God; because they serve those necessities that God has made, and yet made no provisions for them but by their ministry. So that no man can complain that his calling takes him off from religion, his calling itself, and his very worldly employment, is a serving of God; and if it be pursued, according to the rules of Christian prudence, will leave void spaces enough for prayers and retirements of a more spiritual religion.

God has given every man work enough to do that there is no room for idleness; and yet has so ordered the world that there is space for devotion. He who has the fewest businesses of the world, is called upon to spend more time in the dressing of his soul. And he who has the most affairs, may so order them that they shall be a service to God; at certain periods, they are blessed with prayers and actions of religion, and all day long are hallowed by a holy intention. And so long as idleness is quite shut out from our lives, all the sins of wantonness, softness, and effeminacy are prevented. Therefore, to a busy man temptations are fain to climb up together with his business, and sins creep upon him only by accidents and occasions; whereas to an idle person they come in a full body, and with open violence and restless importunity.

Idleness is called "the sin of Sodom and her daughters," and, indeed, is the burial of a living man; an idle person being so useless to any purposes of God and man that he is like one who is dead: he only lives to spend his time and eat the fruits of the earth. He is like a vermin or a wolf, when their time comes they die and perish, and in the meantime do no good; they neither plough nor carry burdens, all they do either is unprofitable or mischievous.

Idleness is the greatest prodigality in the world. It throws away that which is invaluable, in respect of its present use, and irreparable when it is past. But the way to secure and improve our time we may practice in the following rules.

Rules for Employing Our Time

1. In the morning, when you awake, accustom yourself to think first on God. At night also, let him close your eyes. And let your sleep be necessary and healthful, not beyond the needs of nature.

2. Let every man who has a calling be diligent in it, so as not to neglect it in any of those times which are usually and by the custom of prudent persons and good husbands employed in it.

3. Let all the intervals or void spaces of time be employed in prayers, reading, meditating, charity, and means of spiritual and corporal health; ever remembering so to work in our calling, as not to neglect the work of our high calling, but to begin and end the day with God.

4. Avoid the company of busy-bodies and all such as are apt to talk much to little purpose; for no man can be provident of his time who is not prudent in the choice of his company. And if one of the speakers is trifling, he who hears and he who answers are equal losers of their time.

5. Never talk with any man, or undertake any employment, merely to pass the time away. And remember, the time you trifle away was given you to repent in, to pray for pardon of sins, to work out your salvation, to do the work of grace, to lay up

against the Day of Judgment a treasure of good works, that your time may be crowned with eternity.

6. In the midst of the works of your calling, often retire to God in short prayers and exclamations, and those may make up the lack of those larger portions of time which it may be you desire for devotion; for so you reconcile the outward and your inward calling, the church and the commonwealth, the employment of the body and the interest of your soul.

7. Let your employment be such as may become a reasonable person. There are some trades that wholly serve the ends of idle persons and fools, and such as are fit to be seized upon by the severity of laws and banished from under the sun.

8. Let our employment be such as becomes a Christian; that is, in no sense mingled with sin; for he who takes pains to serve the ends of covetousness, or ministers to another's lust, or keeps a shop of impurities or intemperance, is idle in the worst sense; for every hour so spent runs him backward, and must be spent again in the remaining part of his life, and spent better.

9. Let all persons, of all conditions, avoid all delicacy and niceness in their clothing or diet, because such softness engages them upon great misspending of their time, while they dress and comb out all opportunities of their morning devotion, and sleep out the care and provision for their souls.

10. Let every one, of every condition, avoid curiosity, and all inquiry into things that concern them not. For all business in things that concern us not, is an employing our time to no good of ours; and therefore not in order to a happy eternity. In this account our neighbors' necessities are not to be reckoned, for they concern us as one member is concerned in the grief of another; but going from house to house, tattlers and busybodies, who are the canker and rust of idleness, as idleness is the rust of time, are reproved by the apostle in severe language.

11. As much as may be, cut off all impertinent and useless employments of your life: unnecessary visits, long waiting upon great personages, where neither duty nor necessity nor charity

obliges us; all vain meetings, all laborious trifles, and whatsoever spends much time to no real, religious, or charitable purpose.

12. Set apart some portions of every day for more solemn devotion, which be exact in observing; and if variety of employment press upon you, yet so order your rule that the necessary parts of it be not omitted; and though just occasions may make your prayers shorter, yet let nothing but a violent, sudden, and impatient necessity make you, upon any one day, wholly omit your morning and evening devotions.

13. Do not the work of God negligently and idly. Let not your heart be upon the world, when your hand is lifted up in prayer; and be sure to prefer an action of religion in its place, before all worldly pleasure; letting secular things (that may be dispensed within themselves) in these circumstances wait upon the other. In honoring God and doing his work, put forth all your strength, for of that time only you may be most confident that it is gained which is prudently and zealously spent in God's service.

14. When the clock strikes, it is good to say a short prayer every hour, that the parts and returns of devotion may be the measure of your time; and do so also in all the breaches of your sleep, that those spaces which have in them no direct business of the world may be filled with religion.

15. Let him who is most busied set apart some solemn time every year, in which, quitting all worldly business, he may attend wholly to fasting and prayer, and the dressing of his soul by confessions, meditations, and attendance upon God; that he may make up his accounts, renew his vows, make amends for his carelessness, and retire back again from whence levity and the vanities of the world, or the opportunity of temptation, or the distraction of secular affairs have carried him.

16. We shall find the work easier if, before we sleep every night, we examine the actions of the past day with a particular scrutiny. Let us take care that we sleep not without such a recollection of the actions of the day.

17. Let all these things be done prudently and moderately, not with scruple and vexation. For these are good advantages, but the particulars are not divine commandments, and therefore are to be used as shall be found expedient to every one's condition.

Section II

The Second General Instrument of Holy Living: Purity of Intention

That we should intend God's glory in every action we do, is expressed by St. Paul, "Whether you eat or drink, do all to the glory of God" (1 Cor. 10:31). This rule when we observe, is that every action of nature becomes religious, and every meal is an act of worship, and shall have its reward in its proportion, as well as an act of prayer. Blessed be that goodness and grace of God, which, out of infinite desire to glorify mankind, would make the very works of nature capable of becoming acts of virtue, that all our lifetime we may do him service. This grace is so excellent, that it sanctifies the most common action of our life; and yet, so necessary, that without it the very best actions of our devotion are vicious. For he who prays out of custom, or gives alms for praise, or fasts to be accounted religious, is but a Pharisee in his devotion, and a beggar of his alms, and a hypocrite in his fasts; but a holy end sanctifies all these and all other actions which can be made holy. For, as to know the end distinguishes a man from a beast; so to choose a good end distinguishes him from an evil man.

Hezekiah repeated his good deeds upon his sick bed and obtained favor of God; but the Pharisee was accounted insolent for doing the same thing, because this man did it to upbraid his brother, the other to obtain a mercy of God. Holy intention is to the actions of a man that which the soul is to the body, or the root to the tree, or the sun to the world; for without these the body is a dead trunk, the tree is a block, the world is darkness, and the action is sinful.

Rules for Our Intentions

1. In every action reflect upon the end; and in your undertaking of it, consider why you do it, and what you propound to yourself for a reward, and to your action as its end.

2. Begin every action in the name of the Father, of the Son, and of the Holy Spirit; the meaning of which is (a) that we be careful that we do not do the action without the permission or warrant of God; (b) that we design it for the glory of God, if not in the direct action, yet at least in its consequence; and (c) that it may be so blessed that what we intend for innocent and holy purposes may not, by any abuse, be turned into evil, or made the occasion of sin.

3. Let every action of importance begin with prayer, that God would not only bless the action, but also sanctify your purpose, and make an offering of the action to God; holy and well-intended actions being the best offerings we can make to God.

4. In the execution of the action, renew and rekindle your purpose by short prayers, to these purposes, "Not unto us, O Lord, not unto us, but unto your name let all praise be given" (Ps. 115:1), and consider, "Now I am working the work of God, I am his servant, I am in a happy employment, I am doing my Master's business, I am not at my own disposal, I am using his talents, and all the gain must be his." For then be sure, as the glory is his, so the reward shall be yours. If you bring his goods home with increase, he will make you ruler over cities.

5. Take care, that while the altar thus sends up a holy fume, you do not suffer the birds to come and carry away the sacrifice; that is, let not that which began well, and was intended for God's glory, decline and end in your own praise or temporal satisfaction.

6. In every more solemn action of religion, join together many good ends, that the consideration of them may entertain all your affections; and that when any one ceases, the purity of your intention may be supported by another supply. He who fasts only to tame a rebellious body, when he is provided of a remedy, may be tempted to leave off his fasting. But he who

in his fast intends the mortification of every unruly appetite, and to accustom himself to bear the yoke of the Lord, seeking a contempt of the pleasures of meat and drink, humiliation of all wilder thoughts, obedience and humility, austerity and charity, and the convenience and assistance to devotion; whatever happens, will have reason enough to make him to continue his purpose.

7. If any temptation should happen in a religious duty, do not presently omit the action, but rather strive to rectify your intention and to mortify the temptation. Saint Bernard taught us this rule. For when the devil, observing him to preach excellently, tempted him to vainglory, hoping that the good man, to avoid that, would cease preaching, he gave this answer, "I neither began for you, neither for you will I make an end."

Section III

The Third General Instrument of Holy Living: The Practice of the Presence of God

That God is present in all places; that he sees every action, hears all discourses, and understands every thought; is no strange thing to the ear of a Christian, who has been taught this doctrine not only by right reason, and the consent of all the wise men in the world, but also by God himself in Holy Scripture. "'Am I a God at hand,' says the Lord, 'and not a God afar off? Can any hide himself in secret places that I shall not see him?' says the Lord. 'Do not I fill heaven and earth?'" (Jer. 23:23–24). "Neither is there any creature that is not manifest in his sight; but all things are naked and open to the eyes of him to whom we must give account. . . . For in him we live, and move, and have our being" (Heb. 4:13; Acts 17:28). God is wholly in every place, included in no place, not bound with cords (except those of love); not divided into parts, not changeable into several shapes; filling heaven and earth with his present power, and with his never absent nature.

We understand the presence of God in several manners, and to several purposes:

1. God is present by his essence, which, because it is infinite, cannot be contained within the limits of any place.

2. God is everywhere present, by his power. He rolls the orbs of heaven with his hand; he fixes the earth with his foot; he guides all the creatures with his eye, and refreshes them with his influence. He makes the powers of hell to shake with his terrors, and binds the devils with his word, and throws them out with his command, and sends the angels on embassies with his decrees. He hardens the joints of infants, and confirms the bones when they are fashioned beneath secretly in the earth. It is he who assists at the numerous productions of fish; and there is no hollowness in the bottom of the sea, but he shows himself to be Lord of it, by sustaining there the creatures that dwell in it.

3. God is more especially present in some places by the more special manifestations of himself to extraordinary purposes by glory. Thus his seat is in heaven, because there he sits encircled with all the outward demonstrations of his glory, which he is pleased to show to all the inhabitants of his inward and secret courts.

4. God is, by grace and benediction, especially present in holy places, and in the solemn assemblies of his servants. If holy people meet in caves and dens of the earth, when persecution disturbs the public order, God fails not to come there to them.

5. God is especially present in the hearts of his people by his Holy Spirit; and, indeed, the hearts of holy men are temples in the truth of things, and in type and shadow they are heaven itself. For God reigns in the hearts of his servants; there is his kingdom. The power of grace has subdued all his enemies; there is his power. They serve him night and day, and give him thanks and praise; that is his glory. This is the religion and worship of God in the temple.

The temple itself is the heart of man. Christ is the High Priest, who from there sends up the incense of prayers, and joins them to his own intercession, and presents all together to his Father; and the Holy Spirit, by his dwelling there, has also consecrated it into a temple; and God dwells in our hearts by faith, and Christ by his Spirit, so that we are also cabinets of the mysterious Trinity; and what is this short of heaven itself, but as infancy is short of manhood? The same state of life it is, but not the same age. It is heaven in a looking glass—dark, but yet true—representing the beauties of the soul, and the graces of God, and the images of his eternal glory by the reality of a special presence.

6. God is especially present in the consciences of all persons, good and bad, by way of testimony and judgment. That is, he is there a reminder to call our actions to mind, a witness to bring them to judgment, and a judge to acquit or to condemn. And although this manner of presence is in this life after the manner of this life; that is, imperfect, and we forget many actions of our lives; yet the greatest changes of our state of grace or sin, our most considerable actions are always present, like capital letters to an aged and dim eye. And at the Day of Judgment God will draw aside the cloud, and manifest this manner of his presence more notoriously, and make it appear that he was an observer of our very thoughts; and that he only laid those things by, which because we were covered with dust and negligence, were not then discerned. But when we have risen from our dust and imperfection, they will all appear plain and legible.

The consideration of this great truth is of a universal use in the whole life of a Christian. He who remembers that God stands as a witness and a judge, beholding every secrecy, besides his impiety, must have put on impudence, if he is not much restrained in his temptation to sin. For the greatest part of sin is taken away if a man has a witness of his conversation. And he is a great despiser of God who sends a boy away when he is going to commit fornication, and yet will dare to do it, though he knows God is present, and cannot be sent off. As if the eye of a little boy were more awful than the all-seeing eye of God. He is to be feared in public; he is to be feared in private. If you go forth, he spies you; if you go in, he sees you. When you light the candle, he observes you; when you put it out, then also God marks you. Be sure that while you are in his sight, you behave yourself as becomes so holy a presence. But if you will sin, retire yourself wisely, and go where God cannot see; for nowhere else can you be safe.

If men would always consider this, that God is the great eye of the world, always watching over our actions, and an ever-open ear to hear all our words, and an unwearied arm ever lifted up to crush a sinner into ruin; it would be the readiest way in the world to make sin cease from amongst the children of men, and for men to approach to the blessed estate of the saints in heaven, who cannot sin, for they always walk in the presence and behold the face of God.

Rules for Exercising This Consideration

1. Let this actual thought often return, that God is omnipresent, filling every place, and say with David, "Where shall I go from your Spirit, or where shall I flee from your presence? If I ascend up into heaven, you are there; if I make my bed in hell, you are there" (Ps. 139:7–8). It is a great inducement to act faultlessly, when we act before the Judge, who is infallible in his sentence, all knowing in his information, severe in his anger, powerful in his providence, and intolerable in his wrath and indignation.

2. In the beginning of actions of religion, make an act of adoration; that is, solemnly worship God, and place yourself in God's presence, and behold him with the eye of faith, and let your desires actually fix on him as the object of your worship, and the reason of your hope, and the fountain of your blessing. For when you have placed yourself before him and knelt in his presence, it is most likely that all the following parts of your devotion will be answerable to the wisdom of such an apprehension and the glory of such a presence.

3. Let everything you see represent to your spirit the presence, the excellency, and the power of God, and let your conversation with the creatures lead you unto the Creator; for so shall your actions be done more frequently with an actual eye to God's presence, by your often seeing him in the glass of the creation. In the face of the sun you may see God's beauty; in the

fire you may feel his heat warming; in the water his gentleness to refresh you. He it is who comforts your spirits when you have taken cordials. It is the dew of heaven that makes your field give you bread; and the breasts of God are the bottles that minister drink to your necessities. This philosophy, which is obvious to every man's experience, is a good advantage to our piety; and by this act of understanding, our wills are checked from violence and misdemeanor.

4. In your retirement make frequent colloquies or short discourses between God and your own soul. "Seven times a day do I praise you: and in the night season also I thought upon you while I was waking." So did David. And every act of complaint or thanksgiving, every act of rejoicing or of mourning, every petition and every return of the heart in these interactions, is a going to God, an appearing in his presence, and a representing him present to your spirit and to your necessity. And this was long since by a spiritual person called, "a building to God, a chapel in our heart." It reconciles Martha's employment with Mary's devotion, charity, and religion; the necessities of our calling and the employments of devotion. For thus in the midst of the works of your trade, you may retire into your chapel (your heart), and converse with God.

5. Represent and offer to God acts of love and fear, which are the proper effects of this apprehension, and the proper exercise of this consideration. For as God is everywhere present by his power, he calls for reverence and godly fear. As he is present to you in all your needs, and relieves them, he deserves your love; and since in every circumstance of our lives we find one or other of these apparent, and in most things we see both, it is a proper return, that to every such demonstration of God, we express, ourselves sensible of it, by admiring the divine goodness, or trembling at his presence, ever obeying him because we fear to offend him. This is that which Enoch did, who thus walked with God.

6. Let us remember that God is in us, and that we are in him. We are his workmanship, let us not deface it; we are in his presence, let us not pollute it by unholy actions. God has also

"wrought all our works in us" (Isa. 26:12), and because he rejoices in his own works, if we defile them and make them unpleasant to him, we walk perversely with God, and he will walk crookedly toward us.

7. God is in the heart of your brother; refresh him when he needs it, and then you give your alms in the presence of God, and to God, and he feels the relief which you provide for your brother.

8. God is in every place; suppose it therefore to be a church. And that decency of behavior, which you are taught to use in churches, the same use in all places with this difference only: in churches let your actions be religious in external forms also; but there and everywhere let it be religious in abstaining from spiritual indecencies, and in readiness to do good.

9. God is in every creature. Be cruel toward none, neither use any by intemperance. Remember that the creatures and every member of your own body is one of the lesser cabinets and receptacles of God. They are such that God has blessed with his presence, hallowed by his touch, and separated from unholy use by making them belong to his dwelling.

10. He walks as in the presence of God who converses with him in frequent prayer, who runs to him in all his necessities, who asks counsel of him in all his doubts, who opens all his wants to him, who weeps before him for his sins, who asks support for his weakness, who fears him as a Judge, reverences him as a Lord, obeys him as a Father, and loves him as a Patron.

II.

OF CHRISTIAN SOBRIETY

Section I

Of Sobriety in the General Sense

Christian religion, in all it moral parts, is nothing else but the law of nature and reason, complying with the necessities of all the world, and promoting the profit of all relations, and carrying us to that end which God has from eternal ages purposed for all who live according to it, which he has revealed in Jesus Christ; and according to the apostle, has but these three parts: (1) sobriety, (2) justice, and (3) religion. "For the grace of God bringing salvation has appeared to all men, teaching us that denying ungodliness and worldly lusts, we should live *soberly*, *righteously*, and *godly* in this present world, looking for that blessed hope, and glorious appearing of the great God and our Savior Jesus Christ" (Titus 2:11–13). The first contains all our behavior in our private capacities, the fair treating of our bodies and spirits. The second enlarges our duty in all relations to our neighbor. The third contains the offices of direct religion and dealings with God.

Christian sobriety is all the duty that concerns us in the matters of meat and drink, and pleasures and thoughts;

and it has within it the duties of (1) temperance, (2) chastity, (3) humility, (4) modesty, and (5) contentedness.

General Rules of Sobriety

1. Accustom yourself to cut off all superfluity in the provisions of your life; for our desires will enlarge forever. If therefore you suffer them to extend beyond the measures of necessity, they will still swell. But you reduce them to a little compass, when you make nature to be your limit.

2. Suppress your sensual desires in their first approach, for then they are least, and your faculties are stronger. But if they, in their weakness, prevail upon your strength, there will be no resisting them when they are increased, and your abilities lessened. You shall scarce obtain of them to end, if you suffer them to begin.

3. Divert them with some laudable employment.

4. Look upon pleasures not as they come toward you to be enjoyed, but when they begin to go off. The same thing we may do by reason that we do by experience, if either we will look upon pleasures as we are sure they look when they go off, after their enjoyment, or if we will credit the experience of those men who have tasted them and loathed them.

5. Often contemplate the joys of heaven, that when they have filled your desires, which are the sails of your soul, you may steer only there, and never more look back to Sodom. And when your soul dwells above, and looks down upon the pleasures of the world, they seem, like things at a distance, little and contemptible.

Section II

Of Temperance in Eating and Drinking

Sobriety is the bridle of desire, and temperance is the bit of that bridle; a restraint put into a man's mouth, a moderate use of meat and drink, so as may best consist with his health, and may not hinder but help the works of the soul. Temperance is exercised about eating and drinking, and permits the use of them only as they minister to lawful ends; it does not eat and drink for pleasure, but for need and for refreshment. And then God, who gave us such variety of creatures, and our choice to use which we will, may receive glory from our temperate use and thanksgiving; and we may use them indifferently without making them become snares to us, either by too licentious a use of them or too scrupulous a fear of using them at all.

Measures of Temperance in Eating

1. Eat not before the time; unless necessity, or charity, or any intervening circumstance should happen. Remember it had almost cost Jonathan his life because he tasted a little honey before the sun went down, contrary to the king's commandment; and although the great need, which he had, excused him from the sin of gluttony, yet it is inexcusable when you eat before the usual time, and thrust your hand into the dish unseasonably, out of greediness of the pleasure, and impatience of the delay.

2. Eat not delicately or nicely. It is lawful to comply with a weak stomach, but not with a nice and curious palate. When our health requires it, that ought to be provided for; but not our sensuality. Whatsoever is set before you, eat; if it is provided for you, you may eat it, be it never so delicate; and be it plain and common, so it is wholesome and fit for you, it must not be refused upon curiosity—for every degree of that is a degree of intemperance.

3. Eat not too much. Load neither your stomach nor your understanding. Drunkenness is an immoderate use of drink. I call immoderate that which is besides or beyond that order of good things for which God has given us the use of drink. The ends are digestion of our meat, cheerfulness, and refreshment of our spirits, or any end of health. Besides which if we go, or at any time beyond it, it is inordinate and criminal; it is the vice of drunkenness.

Rules for Obtaining Temperance

1. Be not often at feasts, nor at all in dissolute company, when it may be avoided. For variety of pleasing objects steals away the heart of man and company is either violent or enticing, and we are weak or complying. But if you are unavoidably engaged therein, let not mistaken civility or good nature persuade you either to the temptation of staying (if you understand your weakness), or the sin of drinking inordinately.

2. Be severe in your judgment concerning your proportions, and let no occasion make you enlarge far beyond your ordinary. For a man is surprised by parts; and while he thinks one glass more will not make him drunk, that one glass has disabled him from well discerning his present condition and near danger.

3. Propound to yourself (if you are in a capacity), a constant rule of living, of eating and drinking. And, though it may not be fit to observe scrupulously, lest it become a snare to your conscience, yet let not your rule be broke often nor much, but upon great necessity and in small degrees.

4. Never urge any man to eat or drink beyond his own desires. He who does otherwise is drunk with his brother's excess, and reels and falls with his intemperance; that is, the sin of drunkenness is upon both their scores, they both lie wallowing in the guilt.

5. Use St. Paul's instruments of sobriety: "Let us who are of the day be sober, putting on the breastplate of faith and love, and for a helmet the hope of salvation" (1 Thess. 5:8). Faith, hope, and charity are the best weapons in the world to fight against intemperance.

6. As a pursuance of this rule, it is very good advice, that as we begin and end all our times of eating with prayer and thanksgiving, so at the meal we remove and carry up our minds to the celestial table, often thinking of it, and often desiring it; that by enkindling our desires to heavenly banquets, we may be less passionate for the earthly.

7. In all cases, be careful that you are not brought under the power of such things as otherwise are lawful. "All things are

lawful for me . . . but I will not be brought under the power of any" (1 Cor. 6:12), said St. Paul. And to be impatiently desirous of any thing, so that a man cannot abstain from it, is to lose a man's liberty, and to become a servant of meat and drink, or smoke. And I wish this last instance were more considered by persons who little suspect themselves guilty of intemperance.

Section III

Of Chastity

Reader, stay, and do not read the advices of the following section, unless you have a chaste spirit, or desire to be chaste. For there are some spirits so wholly possessed with a spirit of uncleanness, that they turn the most prudent discourses into dirt and filthy apprehensions, like choleric stomachs, changing their very cordials into bitterness, and in a literal sense, "turning the grace of God into wantonness." I have used all the care I could, in the following periods, that I might neither be lacking to assist those that need it, nor yet minister any occasion of fancy to those that need them not. If any man will snatch the pure taper from my hand, and hold it to the devil, he will only burn his own fingers, but shall not rob me of the reward of my good intention.

Chastity is that duty which was mystically intended by God in the law of circumcision. It is the circumcision of the heart, the cutting off all superfluity of naughtiness, and a suppression of all irregular desires in the matter of sensual pleasure. I call all desires irregular and sinful that are not sanctified, 1) by being within the protection of marriage, 2) by being within the order of nature, and 3) by being within the moderation of Christian modesty. Against the first are fornication, adultery, and all voluntary pollutions of either sex. Against the second are all unnatural lusts and incestuous mixtures. Against the third is all immoderate use of permitted beds, concerning which judgment is to be made as concerning meats and drinks; there being no certain degree prescribed to all persons, but it is to be ruled as the other actions of a man, by proportion to the end, by the dignity of the person in the honor and severity of being a Christian, and by other circumstances, of which I am to give account.

Chastity is that grace which forbids and restrains all these, keeping the body and soul pure in that state in which it is placed by God, whether of the single or of the married life. Concerning which our duty is thus described by St. Paul, "For this is the will of God, even your sanctification, that you should abstain from fornication; that every one of you should know how to possess his vessel in sanctification and honor: not in the passion of lust, even as the Gentiles who know not God" (1 Thess. 4:3–5).

Chastity is either abstinence or continence. Abstinence is the duty of virgins or widows; continence of married persons. Chaste marriages are honorable and pleasing to God. Widowhood is pitiable in its solitariness, but amiable and comely when it is adorned with gravity and purity. But virginity is a life of angels, the enamel of the soul, the huge advantage of religion, the great opportunity for the retirements of devotion. And being empty of cares it is full of prayers; being unmingled with the world, it is apt to converse with God; and by not feeling the warmth of nature, flames out with holy fires, till it be burning like the cherubim and the most euphoric order of holy and unpolluted spirits.

Virginity of itself is not a state more acceptable to God; but that which is chosen in order to the conveniences of religion, and is therefore better than the married life, not that it is more holy, but that it is a freedom from cares, an opportunity to spend more time in spiritual employments; it is not allayed with businesses and attendances upon lower affairs. And if it be a chosen condition to these ends, it contains in it a victory over lusts, and greater desires of religion and self-denial, and therefore is more excellent than the married life, in that degree in which it has greater religion, and a greater mortification, a lesser satisfaction of natural desires, and a greater fullness of the spiritual. And just so it may expect that special reward which God has prepared (besides the crown of all faithful souls) for those "who have not defiled themselves with women, but follow the Virgin Lamb for ever."

But some married persons even in their marriage do better please God than some virgins in their state of virginity. They, by giving great example of conjugal affection, by preserving their faith unbroken, by educating children in the fear of God, by patience and contentedness and holy thoughts and the exercises of virtues proper to that state, do not only please God, but do it in a higher degree than those virgins whose piety is not answerable to their great opportunities and advantages.

Married persons, widows, and virgins are all servants of God and coheirs in the inheritance of Jesus if they live within the restraints and laws of their particular estate: chastely, temperately, justly, and religiously.

Acts of Chastity in General

The acts of chastity in general are these:

1. To resist all unchaste thoughts; at no hand entertaining pleasure in the unfruitful fancies and remembrances of uncleanness, although no desire or resolution is entertained.

2. At no hand to entertain any desire, or any fantastic, imaginative loves; though by shame, or disability, or other circumstances, they be restrained from action.

3. To have a chaste eye and a hand; for it is all one with what part of the body we commit adultery. And if a man let his eye loose, and enjoys the lust of it, he is an adulterer.

4. To have a heart and mind chaste and pure; that is, detesting all uncleanness, disliking all its motions, past actions, circumstances, likenesses, discourses; and this ought to be the chastity of virgins and widows, especially, and generally of all men, according to their several necessities.

5. To discourse chastely; with great care declining all indecencies of language, chastening the tongue, and restraining it with grace.

6. To disapprove, for any after act, all involuntary and natural pollutions. For if a man delights in having suffered any

natural pollution, and with pleasure remembers it, he chooses that which was in itself involuntary; and that which, being natural was innocent, becoming voluntary, is made sinful.

But besides these general acts of chastity that are common to all states of men and women, there are some few things proper to several states.

Acts of Virginal Chastity

1. Virgins must remember that the virginity of the body is not only excellent in order to the purity of the soul. But they must also consider that since they are in some measure in a condition like that of angels, it is their duty to spend much time in angelical employment; for in the same degree that virgins live more spiritually than other persons, in the same degree is their virginity a more excellent state.

2. Virgins must be retired and private. For all freedom and looseness of society is a violence done to virginity, not in its natural, but in its moral capacity. That is, it loses part of its severity, strictness, and opportunity of advantages, by rendering that person public, whose work is religion, whose company is angels, whose thoughts must dwell in heaven, and separate from all mixtures of the world.

3. Virgins have a peculiar obligation to charity, for this is the virginity of the soul; as purity, integrity, and separation are of the body, which doctrine we are taught by St. Peter, "Seeing you have purified your souls in obeying the truth through the Spirit unto unfeigned love of the brethren, see that you love one another with a pure heart fervently" (1 Peter 1:22). For a virgin who consecrates her body to God, and pollutes her spirit with impatience, or inordinate anger, gives him what he most hates—a foul and defiled soul.

4. These rules are necessary for virgins, who offer that state to God, and do not mean to enter into the state of marriage. They who only wait the opportunity of a convenient change are to steer themselves by the general rules of chastity.

Rules for Widows

Widows must remember:

1. That God has now restrained the former license, bound up their eyes, and shut up their hearts in a very narrow compass.

2. It is against public honesty to marry another man so long as a woman is with child by her former husband. And of the same fame it is in a lesser proportion to marry within the year of mourning.

3. A widow must restrain her memory and her fancy, not recalling her former permissions with delight. For then she opens that floodgate which her husband's death and her own sorrow have shut up.

4. A widow who desires her widowhood should be a state pleasing to God, must spend her time as devoted virgins should, in fasting, and prayers, and charity.

Rules for Married Persons

Concerning married persons, besides the keeping of their mutual faith with each other, these particulars are useful to be observed:

1. Although their mutual endearments are safe within the protection of marriage, yet they who have wives or husbands must be as though they had them not; that is, they must have an affection greater to each other than they have to any person in the world, but not greater than they have to God.

2. In their permissions they must be sure to observe the order of nature, and the ends of God. "He is an ill husband who uses his wife as a man treats a harlot," having no other end but pleasure. Concerning which our best rule is, that although in this, as in eating and drinking, there is an appetite to be satisfied, yet since that satisfaction was intended by nature for other ends, it should always be joined with all or one of these ends: "with a desire of children, or to avoid fornication, or to endear each other"; but never with a purpose, either in act or desire, to separate the sensuality from these ends which hallow it.

3. Married persons must keep such modesty and decency of treating each other, that they never force themselves into lust, with arts and unbecoming devices; always remembering that those mixtures are most innocent which are most simple and most natural.

4. It is a duty of matrimonial chastity to be restrained and temperate in the use of their lawful pleasures; concerning which, although no universal rule can be given to all persons, any more than to all bodies one proportion of meat and drink; yet married persons are to estimate the degree of their license according to the following proportions: a) that it be moderate, so as to consist with health; b) that it be so ordered as not to be too expensive of time, that precious opportunity of working out our salvation; and c) that it be with a temperate affection, without violent transporting desires, or too sensual applications.

Concerning which a man is to make judgment by proportion to other actions, and the severities of his religion, and the sentences of sober and wise persons; always remembering that marriage is a provision for supply, of the natural necessities of the body, not for the artificial appetites of the mind. And it is a sad truth, that many married persons, thinking that the floodgates of liberty are set wide open without measure or restraints, have felt the final rewards of intemperance and lust, by their unlawful using of lawful permissions. Only let each of them be temperate, and both of them be modest.

5. Married persons, by consent, are to abstain from their mutual entertainments, at solemn times of devotion; not as a duty necessary unto itself, but as being the most proper act of purity, which in their condition they can present to God, and being a good advantage for attending their preparation for the solemn duty. It is St. Paul's counsel, that "by consent for a time they should abstain, that they might give themselves to fasting and prayer" (1 Cor. 7:5).

6. It were well if married persons would, in their penitential prayers, and in their general confessions, suspect themselves; and accordingly, ask a general pardon for all their indecencies, and more passionate applications of themselves, in the offices

of marriage; that what is lawful and honorable in its kind, may not be sullied with imperfect circumstances; or if it be, it may be made clean by repentance.

But, because of all the dangers of a Christian, none are more pressing and troublesome than the temptations to lust; therefore it concerns all who would be safe from this death, to arm themselves by the following rules.

Remedies against Uncleanness

1. When a temptation of lust assaults you, do not resist it by heaping arguments against it and disputing with it, but flee from it. If you hear it speak, though but to dispute with it, it ruins you; and the very arguments you go about to answer, leave a relish upon the tongue.

2. Avoid idleness and fill up all the spaces of your time with severe and useful employment; for lust usually creeps in at those empty places where the soul is unemployed and the body at ease. But of all employments, bodily labor is most useful and of greatest benefit for the driving away the devil.

3. Give no entertainment to the beginnings, the first motions, and secret whispers of the spirit of impurity. For, if you totally suppress it, it dies; if you permit the furnace to breathe its smoke, and flame out at any vent, it will rage to the consumption of the whole.

4. Hard usage of the body has by all ages been accounted of some profit against the spirit of fornication. A spare diet, and a thin coarse table, seldom refreshment, frequent fasts; by such cutting off the provisions of victuals, we shall weaken the strength of our enemy. To which if we add lying upon the ground, painful postures in prayer; and (if the lust be upon us, and sharply tempting), inflicting any smart to overthrow the strongest passion by the most violent pain, we shall find case for the present; and this was St. Paul's remedy, "I bring my body under" (1 Cor. 9:27).

But it was a great nobleness of chastity, which St. Jerom reports of a son of the king of Nicomedia, who being tempted upon flowers and a perfumed bed, with a soft violence, but yet tied down to the temptation, lest the easiness of his posture should abuse him, spit out his tongue into her face; to represent that no virtue has cost the saints so much as this of chastity.

5. Flee from all occasions, temptations, looseness of company, balls and reveling, dances, idle talk, private society with women, staring upon a beauteous face, the company of women who are singers, feasts and liberty, wine and strong drinks, which are made to persecute chastity; ever remembering that it is easier to die for chastity, than to live with it.

6. He who will secure his chastity must first cure his pride and his rage. For oftentimes lust is the punishment of a proud man, to tame the vanity of his pride by the shame of unchastity; and the same intemperate heat that makes anger, enkindles lust.

7. If you are assaulted with an unclean spirit, do not trust yourself alone; but run forth into company, whose reverence and modesty may suppress, or whose society may divert your thoughts; and a perpetual witness of your conversation is of special use against this vice, which evaporates in the open air, being impatient of light and witnesses.

8. Use frequent and earnest prayers to the King of purities, the first of Virgins, the eternal God, who is of essential purity; that he will be pleased to reprove and cast out the unclean spirit.

9. These remedies are of universal efficacy in all cases extraordinary and violent; but in ordinary and common, the remedy which God has provided, that is, honorable marriage, has a natural efficacy, besides a virtue, by the divine blessing, to cure the inconveniencies which otherwise might afflict persons temperate and sober.

Section IV

Of Humility

Humility is the great ornament and jewel of the Christian religion, that whereby it is distinguished from all the wisdom of the world; it not having been taught by the wise men of the Gentiles, but first made part of religion by our Lord Jesus Christ, who propounded himself irritable by his disciples so notably in nothing as in the twin sisters of meekness and humility. "Learn of me, for I am meek and humble, and you shall find rest unto your souls" (Matt. 11:29). And all the world, all that we are, and all that we have; our bodies and our souls, our actions and our sufferings, our conditions at home, our circumstances abroad; our many sins, and our seldom virtues, are so many arguments to make our souls dwell low in the deep valley of humility.

Acts and Offices of Humility

Humility is exercised by the following rules:

1. Whatsoever evil you say of yourself, be content that others should think to be true. And if you call yourself fool, be not angry if another says so of you. For if you think so truly, all men in the world desire other men to be of their opinion; and he is a hypocrite who accuses himself before others, with an intent not to be believed. But he who calls himself intemperate, foolish, and lustful, and is angry when his neighbors call him so, is both a false and a proud person.

2. Love to be concealed and little esteemed. Be content to lack praise, never being troubled when you are slighted or undervalued; for you cannot undervalue yourself, and if you think so meanly as there is reason, no contempt will seem unreasonable.

3. Never be ashamed of your birth, or your parents, or your trade, or your present employment, for the meanness or poverty of any of them; and when there is an occasion to speak of them, such an occasion as would invite you to speak of anything that pleases you, omit it not; but speak as readily and indifferently of your lowliness as of your greatness. Primislaus, the first king of Bohemia, kept his country shoes always by him, to remember from whence he was raised. And Agathocles, by the furniture of his table, confessed that from a potter he was raised to be the king of Sicily.

4. Never speak anything directly tending to your praise, that is, with a purpose to be commended, and for no other end. If other ends be mingled with your honor, as if the glory of God, or charity or necessity, or anything of prudence is your end, you

are not tied to omit your discourse, or your design, that you may avoid praise; but pursue your end, though praise come along in the company. Only let not praise be the design.

5. Take no content in praise when it is offered you; but, let your rejoicing in God's gift be allayed with fear, lest this good bring you to evil.

6. Make no suppletories to yourself, when you are disgraced or slighted, by pleasing yourself with supposing you did deserve praise, though they understood you not, or enviously detracted from you. Neither get to yourself a private theater and flatterers, in whose praises you may keep up your own good opinion of yourself.

7. Be content that he should be applauded, and you laid by as unprofitable; his sentence approved, yours rejected; that he should be preferred, and you fixed in a low employment.

8. Never compare yourself with others, unless it is to advance them, and to depress yourself. To which purpose we must be sure in some sense or other to think ourselves the worst in every company in which we come: one is more learned than I am, another is more prudent, a third more honorable, a fourth more chaste, or he is more charitable, or less proud. For the humble man observes their good, and reflects only upon his own vileness; or considers the many evils of himself, certainly known to himself; and the ill of others, but by uncertain report. Or he considers that the evils done by another are out of much infirmity or ignorance, but his own sins are against a clearer light; and if the other had had such great helps, he would have done more good and less evil. Or he remembers that his old sins, before his conversion, were greater in the nature of the thing, or in certain circumstances, than the sins of other men.

9. Be not always ready to excuse every oversight, or indiscretion, or ill action. But if you are guilty of it, confess it plainly; for virtue scorns a lie for its cover; but to hide a sin with it, is like a crust of leprosy drawn upon an ulcer. If you are not guilty (unless it be scandalous), be not over earnest to remove it; but rather use it as an argument to chastise all greatness of opinion in yourself; and accustom yourself to bear reproof patiently and

contentedly, and the harsh words of your enemies, as knowing that the anger of an enemy is a better monitor, and represents our faults, or admonishes us of our duty with more heartiness, than the kindness of a friend.

10. Give God thanks for every weakness, deformity, and imperfection, and accept it as a favor and grace of God, and an instrument to resist pride, and nurse humility; ever remembering that when God, by giving you a crooked back, has also made your spirit stoop, you are more ready to enter the narrow gate of heaven than by being straight, and standing upright, and thinking highly. Thus the apostles "rejoiced in their infirmities," not moral, but natural and accidental, in their being beaten and whipped like slaves, in their nakedness and poverty.

11. Be sure never to praise yourself, or to dispraise anyone else, unless God's glory or some holy end does hallow it. And it was noted to the praise of Cyrus, that among his equals in age, he would never play at any sport, or use any exercise, in which he knew himself more excellent than they. But in such in which he was unskillful, he would make his challenges; lest he should shame them by his victory, and that he himself might learn something of their skill, and do them civilities.

Means of Increasing the Grace of Humility

1. Make confession of your sins often to God, and consider what all that evil amounts to, which you then charge upon yourself.

2. Every day call to mind some one of your foulest sins, or the most shameful of your disgraces, or the most indiscreet of your actions, or anything that did then most trouble you, and apply it to the present swelling of your spirit, and it may help to allay it.

3. Pray often for this grace, with all passion of desire, and in your devotion interpose many acts of humility by way of confession and address to God, and reflection upon yourself.

4. Remember that the blessed Savior of the world has done more to prescribe, and transmit, and secure this grace than any other; his whole life being a continued example of

humility, a vast descent from the glorious bosom of his Father to the womb of a poor maiden, to the form of a servant, to the miseries of a sinner, to a life of labor, to a state of poverty, to a death of malefactors, to the grave of death, and the intolerable calamities which we deserved. And it would be a good design, and yet but reasonable, that we should be as humble in the midst of our greatest imperfections and basest sins, as Christ was in the midst of his fullness of the Spirit, and most admirable virtues.

5. Drive away all flatterers from your company, and at no hand endure them.

Section V

Of Modesty

Modesty is the appendage of sobriety, and is to chastity, to temperance, and to humility, as the fringes are to a garment. It is a grace of God that moderates the over-activeness and curiosity of the mind, orders the passions and external actions, and is directly opposed to curiosity, boldness, and indecency. The practice of modesty consists in these following rules.

Acts of Modesty, as It Is Opposed to Curiosity

1. Do not inquire into the secrets of God, but be content to learn your duty, according to the quality of your person or employment, that is plainly, if you are not concerned in the conduct of others; but if you are a teacher, learn it so as may best enable you to discharge your office.

2. Do not inquire into the things that are too hard for you, but learn modestly to know your infirmities and abilities.

3. Let us not inquire into the affairs of others that concern us not; but be busied within ourselves and our own spheres.

4. Never listen at their doors or windows; for besides that it contains in it danger and a snare, it is also invading your neighbor's privacy, and laying that open, which he therefore enclosed, that it might not be open. Never ask what he carries covered so

curiously; for it is enough that it is covered curiously. Here also is reducible, that we never open letters without public authority, or reasonably presumed leave, or great necessity.

Every man has in his own life sins enough, in his own mind trouble enough, in his own fortune evils enough, and in performance of his offices failings more than enough to entertain his own inquiry. So that curiosity after the affairs of others cannot be without envy and an evil mind. Curiosity is the direct incontinency of the spirit; and adultery itself in its principle is many times nothing but a curious inquisition after, and envying of, another man's enclosed pleasures.

Acts of Modesty, as It Is Opposed to Boldness

1. Let us always bear about us such impressions of reverence and fear of God, as to tremble at his voice, to express our apprehensions of his greatness in all great circumstances, in popular judgments, loud thunders, tempests, earthquakes; not only for fear of being smitten ourselves, but also that we may humble ourselves before his almightiness, and express that infinite distance between his infiniteness and our weakness, at such times especially when he gives such visible arguments of it. He who is merry and airy at shore, when he sees a tempest on the sea, or dances briskly when God thunders from heaven, regards not when God speaks to all the world, but is possessed with a firm immodesty.

2. Be reverent, modest, and reserved in the presence of your betters, giving to all according to their quality and their titles of honor; keeping distance, speaking little, answering pertinently, not interposing without leave or reason, not answering to a question propounded to another; and ever present to your superiors the fairest side of your discourse, of your temper, of your ceremony, as being ashamed to serve excellent persons with unhandsome interactions.

3. Never offer to justify what is indeed a fault, but modestly be ashamed of it, ask pardon, and make amends.

4. Do not be confident in an uncertain matter, but report things modestly, according to the degree of persuasion that

ought to be brought about in you by the efficacy of the authority, or the reason inducing you.

5. Do not pretend to more knowledge than you have, but be content to seem ignorant where you are, lest you be either brought to shame, or retire into shamelessness.

Acts of Modesty, as It Is Opposed to Indecency

1. In your prayers, in places of religion, use reverent postures, great attention, and the lowest gestures of humility, remembering that we speak to God, in our reverence to whom we cannot possibly exceed; but that the expression of this reverence be according to law or custom, and the example of the most prudent and pious persons.

2. In all public meetings, private addresses, discourses, and journeys, use those forms of salutations, reverence, and decency which custom prescribes, and is usual amongst the most sober persons; giving honor to whom honor belongs, taking place of none of your betters; and in all cases of question concerning precedency, giving it to anyone that will take it.

3. Toward your parents use all modesty of duty, and humble carriage; toward them and your kindred be severe in the modesties of chastity; ever fearing lest the freedoms of natural kindness should enlarge into any unhandsome neighborhood.

4. Be grave, decent, and modest in your clothing; never let it be above your condition, nor always equal to it; never light or amorous, discovering a nakedness through a thin veil, which you pretend to hide. Remember what becomes a Christian professing holiness, chastity, and the discipline of the holy Jesus.

5. Here also is to be reduced singular and affected walking, proud, nice, and ridiculous gestures of body, painting, and lascivious dressings. Modesty, in this instance, is expressly enjoined to all Christian women by St. Paul, "That women adorn themselves in modest apparel, with propriety and moderation, not with braided hair, or gold, or pearls, or costly array; but (which becomes women professing godliness), with good works" (1 Tim. 2:9–10).

Section VI

Of Contentedness in All States and Circumstances

Virtues and discourses are like friends, necessary in all fortunes; but those are the best which are friends in our sadness, and support us in our sorrows; and in this sense, no man who is virtuous can be friendless; nor has any man reason to complain of the divine providence, or accuse the public disorder of things, since God has appointed one remedy for all the evils in the world, and that is a contented spirit. For this alone makes a man pass through fire, and not be scorched; through seas, and not be drowned; through hunger and nakedness, and lack nothing. He who composes his spirit to the present circumstance has a variety of instances for his virtue, but none to trouble him, because his desires enlarge not beyond his present fortune.

And a wise man is like the center of a wheel in the midst of all the circumvolutions and changes of posture, without violence or change, save that it turns gently in compliance with its changed parts, and is indifferent which part is up and which is down. For there is some virtue or other to be exercised whatever happens, either patience or thanksgiving, love or fear, moderation or humility, charity or contentedness, and they are every one of them equally in order to this great end and felicity. We may be reconciled to poverty and a low fortune, if we suffer contentedness and the grace of God to make the proportion.

1. Contentedness in all states is a duty of religion; it is the great reasonableness of complying with the divine providence, which governs the entire world, and has so ordered us in the administration of his great family. He would be a strange fool who should be angry because dogs and sheep need no shoes, and yet is himself full of care to get some. God has supplied those needs to them by natural provisions, and to you by artificial. For he has given you reason, to learn your trade, or some means to make or buy them, so that it only differs in the manner of the provision; and which would you rather lack, shoes or reason?

And my patron who has given me a farm, is freer to me than if he gives a loaf ready baked. But however, all these gifts come from him, and therefore it is fit he should dispense them as he pleases; and if we murmur here, we may at the next melancholy be troubled that God did not make us to be angels or stars. For if that which we are, or have, does not content us, we may be troubled for everything in the world, which is besides our being or our possessions.

God is the Master of the scenes; we must not choose which part we shall act; it concerns us only to be careful that we do it well; always saying, "If this pleases God, let it be as it is." And we, who pray that God's will may be done in earth as it is in heaven, must remember that the angels do whatever is commanded them, and go wherever they are sent, and refuse no circumstances; and if their employment be crossed by a higher degree, they sit down in peace, and rejoice in the event. When the angel of Judea could not prevail on behalf of the people committed to his charge, because the angel of Persia opposed it; he only told the story at the command of God, and was content, and worshipped with as great an ecstasy in his proportion, as the prevailing spirit. Do so likewise: keep the station where God has placed you, and you shall never long for things without; but sit at home feasting upon the divine providence and your own reason, by which you are taught that it is necessary and reasonable to submit to God.

For, is not all the world God's family? Are we not his creatures? Are we not as clay in the hands of the Potter? Do we not live upon his meat, and move by his strength, and do our work by his light? Are we anything but what we are from him? And shall there be a mutiny among the flocks and herds, because their Lord or their Shepherd chooses their pasture, and suffers not to wander in deserts and unknown ways? If we choose, we do it so foolishly that we cannot like what we have chosen long, and most commonly not at all. But God, who can do what he pleases, is wise to choose safely for us, affectionate to comply with our needs, and powerful to execute all his wise decrees. Here therefore is the wisdom of the contented man, to let God choose for him; for when we have given up our wills to him, and stand in that station of the battle where our great General has placed us, our spirits must need rest, while our conditions have for their security the power, the wisdom, and the love of God.

2. Contentedness in all circumstances brings great peace of spirit, and is the great instrument of temporal felicity. It makes a man depend not upon the uncertain dispositions of men for his well-being, but only on God and his own spirit.

Exercises to Increase Contentedness

1. When anything happens to our displeasure, let us endeavor to take off its trouble by turning it into spiritual advantage and handle it on that side in which it may be useful to the designs of reason. For there is nothing but has a double handle. When an enemy reproaches you, look on him as an impartial relater of your faults, for he will tell you more truly than your fondest friend will. You may call them precious balms, though they break your head, and forgive his anger while you make use of the plainness of his declamation; if there be nothing else in the disgrace but that it makes you walk warily, and tread surely, that is better than to be flattered into pride and carelessness.

2. Never compare your condition with those above you; but look upon those thousands with whom you would not for any interest change your condition. There are but a few kings among mankind, but many thousands who are very miserable if compared to you. However, it is a huge folly rather to grieve for the good of others, than to rejoice for that good which God has given us of our own. And yet there is no wise or good man who would change persons or conditions entirely with any man in the world. It may be he would have one man's wealth added to himself, or the power of a second, or the learning of a third; but still he would receive these into his own person, because he loves that best, and therefore esteems it best, and therefore values all that which he is, before all that which any other man in the world can be. Would any man be Dives, to have his wealth, or Judas for his office, or Saul for his kingdom, or Absalom for his beauty, or Ahithophel for his policy? It is likely he would wish all these, and yet he would be the same person still.

3. It conduces much to our content, if we pass by those things that happen to our trouble, and consider that which is pleasing and prosperous, that by the representation of the better, the worst may be blotted out. And at the worst you have enough to keep you alive, and to keep up and to improve your hopes of heaven. If I am overthrown in my suit at law, yet my house and my land is left me still; or I have a virtuous wife, or hopeful children, or kind friends. If I have lost one child, it may be I have two or three left. Or else reckon the blessings that you have received, and therefore be pleased in the change and variety of affairs to receive evil from the hand of God as well as good.

When sadness lies heavy upon you, remember that you are a Christian, designed for the inheritance of Jesus. And what do you think concerning your lot and portion in eternity? Do you think that you shall be saved or damned? Indeed if you think you shall perish, I do not blame you for being sad, sad till your heartstrings crack, but then, why are you troubled at the loss of your money? What should a damned man do with money? Did ever any man upon the rack afflict himself because he had received a cross answer from his mistress? If you do really believe you shall be damned, I do not say it will cure the sadness of your poverty, but it will swallow it up.

But if you believe you shall be saved, consider how great is that joy, how infinite is that change, how unspeakable is the glory, how excellent is the recompense for all the sufferings in the world. Here you are, but a stranger traveling to your country, where the glories of a kingdom are prepared for you; it is therefore a huge folly to be much afflicted because you have a less convenient inn to lodge in by the way.

Indeed, there is no man but has blessings enough in present possession to outweigh the evils of a great affliction. Tell the joints of your body, and do not accuse the universal providence for a lame leg, or the lack of a finger, when all the rest is perfect, and you have a noble soul, a particle of divinity, the image of God himself; and by the lack of a finger you may the better know how to estimate the remaining parts.

I have fallen into the hands of ill men, and they have taken all from me: what now? Let me look about me. They have left me the sun and moon, fire and water, a loving wife, and many friends to pity me, and some to relieve me; and they have not taken away my cheerful spirit and good conscience. They still have left me the providence of God and all the promises of the gospel, and my religion, and my hopes of heaven, and my charity to them too. Still I sleep and digest, I eat and drink, I read and meditate; I can walk in my neighbor's pleasant fields, and see the varieties of natural beauties, and delight in all that in which God delights, that is, in virtue and wisdom, in the whole creation, and in God himself. And he that has so many causes of joy, and so great, is very much in love with sorrow and peevishness, who loses all these pleasures, and chooses to sit down upon his little handful of thorns; he deserves to starve in the midst of plenty and to lack comfort while he is encircled with blessings.

4. Enjoy the present, whatsoever it be, and be not solicitous for the future. For if you take your foot from the present standing, and thrust it forward toward tomorrow's event, you are in a restless condition. It is like refusing to quench your present thirst by fearing you shall lack drink the next day. If it is well today, it is madness to make the present miserable by fearing it may be ill tomorrow. If tomorrow you shall lack, your sorrow will come time enough, though you do not hasten it. Let your trouble tarry till its own day comes. But if it is ill today, do not increase the affliction by the care of tomorrow.

Enjoy the blessings of this day, if God sends them; and the evils of it bear patiently and sweetly. For this day is only ours, we are dead to yesterday, and we are not yet born to tomorrow. He therefore who enjoys the present, if it is good, enjoys as much as is possible. And if only that day's trouble leans upon him, it is finite. "Sufficient to the day," said Christ, "is the evil thereof" (Matt. 6:34). Sufficient, but not intolerable. But if we look abroad, and bring into one day's thought the evil of many— certain and uncertain, what will be, and what will never be—our load will be as intolerable as it is unreasonable.

5. Let us prepare our minds against changes, always expecting them, that we be not surprised when they come. For nothing is so great an enemy to a contented spirit as unpreparedness and inconsideration; and when our fortunes are changed, our spirits are unchanged, if they always stood in the expectation of sorrows. "O death, how bitter are you to a man that is at rest in his possessions!" And to the rich man who had promised to himself ease and fullness for many years, it was a sad arrest, and his soul was surprised the first night; but the apostles, who every day knocked at the gate of death, and looked upon it continually, went to their martyrdom in peace and evenness.

6. Let us often frame to ourselves the images of those blessings we have, just as we usually understand them when we want them. Consider how desirable health is to a sick man, or liberty to a prisoner; if but a fit of the toothache seizes us with violence, all those troubles, which in our health afflicted us, disband immediately, and seem inconsiderable. He who in his health is troubled that he is in debt, and spends sleepless nights; let him fall into a fit of the stone, or a high fever, and he despises the arrest of all his first troubles, and is a man unconcerned. Remember then that God has given you a blessing, the lack of which would be infinitely more trouble than your present debt, or poverty, or loss; and therefore is now more to be valued in the possession, and ought to outweigh your trouble.

The very blessings of immunity, liberty, and integrity, which we commonly enjoy, deserve the thanksgiving of a whole life. If God should send a cancer upon your face, if he should spread a crust of leprosy upon your skin, what would you give to be but as now you are? Would you not on that condition be as poor as I am, or as the meanest of your brethren? Would you not choose your present loss or affliction as a thing extremely eligible, if you might exchange the other for this? You are free from a thousand calamities, every one of which, if it were upon you, would make you insensible of your present sorrow. And therefore let your joy (which should be as great for your freedom from them, as is your sadness when you feel any of them), effect the same cure upon your discontent. For if we are not extremely foolish or vain, thankless or senseless, a great joy is more apt to cure sorrow and discontent than a great trouble is.

I have known an affectionate wife, when she had been in fear of parting with her beloved husband, heartily desire of God his life, or society, upon any conditions that were not sinful; and choose to beg with him rather than to feast without him. And the same person has, upon that consideration, borne poverty nobly, when God has heard, her prayer in the other matter. What wise man in the world is there who does not prefer a small fortune with peace, before a great one with contention, and war, and violence? Then he is no longer wise if he alters his opinion when he has his wish.

7. If you will secure a contented spirit, you must measure your desires by your fortune, not your fortune by your desires. That is, be governed by your needs, not by your fancy. Is that beast better that has two or three mountains to graze on, than a little bee that feeds on dew or manna, and lives upon what falls every morning from the storehouses of heaven, clouds, and providence? Can a man quench his thirst better from the fountain when it is finely paved with marble, than when it swells over the green turf? Pride and artificial gluttonies do but adulterate nature, making our diet unhealthy, our appetites impatient and insatiable. But that which we miscall poverty, is indeed nature, and its proportions are the just measures of a man, and the best instruments of content.

8. In all troubles let us take sanctuary in religion, and by innocence cast out anchors for our souls, to keep them from shipwreck, though they are not kept from storm. When a man suffers in a good cause, or is afflicted, and yet does not walk perversely with God, then he may say, "Anytus and Melitus may kill me, but they cannot hurt me." Then St. Paul's character is engraved on the forehead of our fortune: "We are troubled on every side, but not distressed; perplexed, but not in despair; persecuted, but not forsaken; cast down, but not destroyed" (2 Cor. 4:8–9). And "who is he that will harm you, if you are followers of that which is good?" (1 Peter 3:13). For

indeed everything in the world is indifferent, but sin. And all the scorching of the sun is very tolerable in respect of the burnings of a fever. The greatest evils are from within us, and from ourselves also we must look for our greatest good; for God is the fountain of it, but reaches it to us by our own hands. And when all things look sadly ruined about us, then only we shall find how excellent a fortune it is to have God for our friend; and of all friendships that only is created to support us in our needs.

9. Consider that a state of affliction is a school of virtue. It reduces our spirits to soberness, and our counsels to moderation; it corrects levity, and interrupts the confidence of sinning. "It is good for me," said David, "that I have been afflicted, for thereby I have learned your law" (Ps. 119:71). And "I know, O Lord, that you of very faithfulness have caused me to be troubled." For God, who in mercy and wisdom governs the world, would never have suffered so much sadness, and have sent them especially to the most virtuous and the wisest men, but that he intends they should be the nursery of virtue, the exercise of wisdom, the trial of patience, the venturing for a crown, and the gate of glory.

10. But some men are highly tempted, and are brought to a strait, that without a miracle they cannot be relieved. What shall they do? Let not any man, by way of impatience, cry out that God will not work a miracle; for God, by a miracle, did give meat and drink to his people in the wilderness, of which he had made no particular promise in any covenant. And, if all natural means fail, it is certain that God will rather work a miracle than break his word; he can do that, he cannot do this. Only we must remember that our portion of temporal things is but food and raiment. God has not promised us coaches and horses, neither has he promised to minister to our needs in such circumstances as we shall appoint, but such as he himself shall choose.

God will enable you to pay your debt (if you beg it of him), or else he will pay it for you; that is, take your desires as a discharge of your duty, and pay it to your creditor in blessings, or in some secret of his providence. It may be he has laid up the corn that shall feed you in the granary of your brother; or will clothe you with his wool. He enabled St. Peter to pay his tax by the ministry of a fish; and Elijah to be waited on by a raven, which was both his minister and his steward for provisions; and his holy Son rode in triumph upon a donkey that grazed in another man's pastures. And if God gives to him the dominion, and reserves the use to you, you have the better half of the two; but the charitable man serves God and serves your need; and both join to provide for you, and God blesses both.

But if he takes away the pots of meat from you, he can also alter the appetite, and he has given you power to restrain it; and if he lessens the revenue, he will also shrink the necessity; or if he gives but a very little, he will make it go a great way; or if he sends you but a coarse diet, he will bless it and make it healthy, and cure all the anguish of your poverty by giving you patience and contentedness. For the grace of God secures provisions for you; and yet the grace of God feeds and supports the spirit in the lack of provisions. And if a thin table is apt to enfeeble the spirits of one used to eating better; yet the cheerfulness of a spirit that is blessed will make a thin table become a delicacy, if the man were as well taught as he was fed, and learned his duty when he received the blessing.

III.

OF CHRISTIAN JUSTICE

Introduction

Justice is, by the Christian religion, enjoined in all its parts by the two following propositions in Scripture: "Whatever you want men to do to you, do also to them" (Matt. 7:12). This is the measure of commutative justice, or of that justice which supposes exchange of things profitable for things profitable; that as I supply your need, you may supply mine; as I do a benefit to you, I may receive one by you. And because every man may be injured by another, therefore his security shall depend upon mine. If he will not let me be safe, he shall not be safe himself (only the manner of his being punished is upon great reason, both by God and all the world, taken from particular individuals and committed to a public disinterested person, who will do justice, without passion, both to him and to me); if he refuses to do me advantage, he shall receive none when his needs require it.

The other part of justice is commonly called distributive, and is commanded in this rule, "Render to all their dues: tribute to whom tribute is due, custom to whom custom, fear to whom fear, honor to whom honor. Owe no man any thing, but to love one another" (Rom. 13:7–8). As the first considers an equality of persons in respect of the contract, or particular necessity, this supposes a difference of persons, and no particular bargains, but such necessary interactions as by the laws of God or man are introduced. I shall reduce all the particulars of both kinds to these four heads: 1) obedience, 2) provision, 3) negotiation, and 4) restitution.

Section I

Of Obedience to Our Superiors

Our superiors are set over us in affairs of the world, or the affairs of the soul, and are called accordingly, ecclesiastical or civil. Toward whom our duty is thus generally described in the New Testament. For civil governors the commands are these: "Render to Caesar the things that are Caesar's" (Mark 12:17); and "Let every soul be subject to the higher powers; for there is no power but of God: the powers that be are ordained of God. Whosoever therefore resists the power, resists the ordinance of God; and those who resist shall receive to themselves damnation" (Rom. 13:1–2). Also, "Put them in mind to be subject to principalities and powers, and to obey magistrates" (Titus 3:1); and, "Submit yourselves to every ordinance of man, for the Lord's sake; whether it be to the king, as supreme, or unto governors, as unto those who are sent by him for the punishment of evildoers, and the praise of those who do well" (1 Peter 2:13–14).

For ecclesiastical governors, thus we are commanded: "Obey those who have the rule over you, and submit yourselves, for they watch for your souls as those who must give an account" (Heb. 13:17); and, "Hold such in reputation" (Phil. 2:29); and, "To this end did I write, that I might know the proof of you, whether you be obedient in all things," said St. Paul to the church of Corinth (2 Cor. 2:9). Our duty is reducible to practice by the following rules.

Duties of Obedience to Superiors

1. We must obey all human laws appointed and constituted by lawful authority; that is, of the supreme power, according to

OF CHRISTIAN JUSTICE 49

the constitution of the place in which we live; all laws, I mean, which are not against the law of God.

2. In obedience to human laws, we must observe the letter of the law where we can, without doing violence to the reason of the law, and the intention of the lawgiver. But where they cross each other, the reason of the law is to be preferred before the letter.

3. If the general reason of the law ceases in our particular, and a contrary reason rises upon us, we are to procure leave to omit the observation of it in such circumstances, if there be any persons appointed for granting it; but if there be none, or if it is not easily to be had, we are dispensed with in the nature of the thing, without further process.

4. As long as the law is obligatory, so long our obedience is due; and he who begins a contrary custom, without reason, sins. But he who breaks the law when the custom is entered and fixed, is excused, because it is supposed the legislative power consents, when by not punishing, it suffers disobedience to grow up to a custom.

5. Obedience to human laws must be for the sake of conscience; that is, because in such obedience public order and benefit is concerned, and because the law of God commands us, therefore we must make a conscience in keeping the just laws of superiors. And although the matter before the making of the law was indifferent, yet now the obedience is not indifferent; but, next to the laws of God, we are to obey the laws of all our superiors.

6. Although from inferior judges we may appeal where the law permits us, yet we must rest in the judgment of the supreme; and if we are wronged, we must complain to God of the injury, not of the persons, and he will deliver us from unrighteous judges.

7. Do not believe you have kept the law, when you have suffered the punishment. For although patiently to submit is a part of obedience, yet this is such a part as supposes another left undone. And the law punishes, not because she is as well

pleased in taking vengeance as in being obeyed, but she uses punishment as a means to secure obedience for the future.

8. Human laws are not to be broken with scandal, nor at all without reason; for he who does it cautiously is a despiser of the law, and undervalues the authority.

9. Pay that reverence to your prince, to the persons of his ministers, of your parents and spiritual guides, which by the customs of the place you live in are usually paid to such persons in their several degrees.

10. Do not lift your hand against your prince or parent, upon any pretense whatsoever; but bear all personal affronts and inconveniencies at their hands, and seek no remedy but by patience and piety, yielding and praying, or absenting yourself.

11. "Speak not evil of the ruler of your people" (Acts 23:5), neither "curse your father or mother" (Matt. 15:4), nor revile your spiritual guides, nor discover and lay naked their infirmities; but treat them with reverence and religion, and preserve their authority sacred by esteeming their persons venerable.

12. Pay tribute and custom to princes according to the laws, and maintenance to your parents according to their necessity, and honorable support to the clergy, according to the dignity of their work, and the customs of the people.

13. Remember always that duty to our superiors is not an act of commutative justice, but of distributive; that is, although kings, and parents, and spiritual guides are to pay a great duty to their inferiors, the duty of their several charges and government; yet the good government of a king and of parents are actions of religion as they relate to God, and of piety as they relate to their people and families. The consequence of which is this, so far as concerns our duty: if princes or parents fail of their duty, we must not fail of ours; for we are answerable to them and to God too, as being accountable to all our superiors, and so are they to theirs. They are above us, and God is above them.

Section II

Of That Part of Justice Which Is Due from Superiors to Inferiors

As God has imprinted his authority in several parts upon several states of men, as princes, parents, spiritual guides; so he has also delegated and committed part of his care and providence unto them, that they may be instrumental in conveying such blessings which God knows we need, and which he intends should be the effects of government. For since God governs all the world as King, provides for us as Father, and is the great Guide of our spirits as the Head of the church, and the great Shepherd and Bishop of our souls; they who have portions of these dignities have also their share of the administration: the sum of all which is usually signified in these two words, *governing* and *feeding*, and is particularly recited in these following rules.

Duties of Kings, and All the Supreme Powers, as Lawgivers

1. Princes of the people, and all who have legislative power, must provide useful and good laws for the defense of propriety, for the encouragement of labor, for the safeguard of their persons, for determining controversies, for reward of noble actions, and excellent arts and rare inventions.

2. Princes must provide that the laws be duly executed, for a good law without execution is like an unperformed promise; and therefore they must be severe exactors of accounts from their delegates and ministers of justice.

3. Princes must be fathers of the people, and provide such instances of gentleness, ease, wealth, and advantages as may make mutual confidence between them. They must fix their security, under God, in the love of the people; which therefore they must, with all arts of sweetness, popularity, nobleness, and sincerity, endeavor to secure to themselves.

The Duty of Superiors as They Are Judges

1. Judges must judge the causes of all persons uprightly and impartially, without any personal consideration of the power of the mighty, or the bribe of the rich, or the needs of the poor.

2. A prince may not, much less may inferior judges, deny justice when it is legally and competently demanded.

The Duty of Parents to Their Children

1. "Fathers, do not provoke your children to wrath" (Eph. 6:4); that is, be tenderhearted, compassionate and gentle, complying with all the innocent infirmities of your children, and in their several ages proportioning to them several usages, according to their needs and their capacities.

2. "Bring them up in the nurture and admonition of the Lord" (Eph. 6:4); that is, season their younger years with pious principles, make them in love with virtue, and make them habitually so before they come to choose or discern good from evil, that their choice may be with less difficulty and danger.

3. Parents must show piety at home; that is, they must give good example and reverent behavior in the face of their children; and all those instances of charity which usually endear each other; sweetness of conversation, affability, frequent admonition, all significations of love and tenderness, care and watchfulness, must be expressed toward children, that they may look upon their parents as their friends and patrons, their defense and sanctuary, their treasure and their guide.

4. Parents must provide for their own, according to their condition, education, and employment; called, by St. Paul, "a laying up for their children"; that is, an enabling them—by competent portions, or good trades, arts, or learning—to defend themselves against the world, that they may not be exposed to temptation, beggary, or unworthy arts.

5. This duty is to extend to a provision of conditions and a state of life. Parents must, according to their power and reason, provide husbands or wives for their children; in which they must secure piety and religion, and the affection and love of

the interested persons; and after these, let them make what provisions they can for other conveniences or advantages, ever remembering that they can do no injury more afflictive to their children than to join them with cords of a disagreeing affection.

Rules for Married Persons

Husbands must give to their wives love, maintenance, duty, and the sweetness of conversation; and wives must pay to them all they have or can, with the interest of obedience and reverence. They must be complicated in affections and interest, that there be no distinction between them of yours and mine. And if the title is the man's or the woman's, yet the use must be common; only the wisdom of the man is to regulate all extravagancies and indiscretions. In other things, no question is to be made; and their goods should be as their children: not to be divided, but of one possession and provision. Whatsoever is otherwise is not marriage, but merchandise.

The husband must rule over the wife, as the soul does over the body: obnoxious to the same sufferings, and bound by the same affections, and doing or suffering by the permissions and interest of each other; that (as the old philosopher said), as the humors of the body are mingled with each other in the whole substance, so marriage may be a mixture of interests, of bodies, of minds, of friends; a conjunction of the whole life, and the noblest of friendships. But if, after all the fair actions, and innocent chaste compliances, the husband is morose and ungentle, let the wife discourse thus: "If, while I do my duty, my husband neglects me, what will he do if I neglect him?"

The Duty of Masters of Families

The same care is to be extended to all of our family in their proportions as to our children. For, as by St. Paul's economy, the heir differs nothing from a servant while he is in minority, so a servant should differ nothing from a child in the substantial part of the care, and the difference is only in degrees. Servants and masters are of the same kindred, and of the same nature, and heirs of the same promises. And, therefore, 1) they must be provided with necessities for their support and maintenance; 2) they must be used with mercy; 3) their work must be tolerable and merciful; 4) their restraints must be reasonable; 5) their religion must be taken care of; and 6) masters must correct their servants with gentleness, prudence, and mercy; not for every slight fault; not always, not with upbraiding and disgraceful language, but with such only as may express and reprove the fault, and amend the person.

But in all these things measures are to be taken by the contract made, by the laws and customs of the place, by the sentence of prudent and merciful men, and by the cautions and remembrances given us by God; such as is written by St. Paul, "as knowing that we also have a Master in heaven" (Col. 4:1). The master must not be a lion in his house, lest his power be obeyed, and his person hated; his eye be waited on, and his business be neglected in secret. No servant will do his duty, unless he makes a conscience of it, or loves his master. If he does it not for God's sake, or his master's, he will not always for his own.

The duty of ministers and spiritual guides to the people is of so great a burden, so various in rules, so intricate and busy with caution, that it requires a distinct tract by itself.

Section III

Of Civil Contracts

This part of justice is such as depends upon the laws of man directly, and upon the laws of God only by consequence; and from civil laws or private agreements it is to take its estimate and measures. And although our duty is plain and easy, requiring of us honesty in contracts, sincerity in affirming, simplicity in bargaining, and faithfulness in performing, yet it may be helped by the addition of these following rules and considerations.

Rules and Measures of Justice in Bargaining

1. In making contracts, do not use many words; for all the business of a bargain is summed up in few sentences; and he who speaks least, means fairest, as having fewer opportunities to deceive.

2. Lie not at all; neither in a little thing nor in a great, neither in the substance nor in the circumstance, neither in word nor deed. That is, pretend not what is false, cover not what is true, and let the measure of your affirmation or denial be the understanding of your contractor. For he who deceives the buyer or the seller, by speaking what is true in a sense not intended or understood by the other, is a liar and a thief. For in bargains, you are to avoid not only what is false, but also that which deceives.

3. Let no prices be heightened by the necessity or unskillfulness of the contractor. For the first is directly uncharitable to the person, and injustice in the thing; and the other is deceit and oppression. Much less must any man make necessities, as by engrossing a commodity, detaining corn, or the like indirect arts; for such persons are unjust to all single persons with whom in such cases they contract, and oppressors of the public.

4. In interactions with others, do not do all that you may lawfully do; but keep something within your power. And because there is a latitude of gain in buying and selling, take not the utmost penny that is lawful, or which you think so; for although it be lawful, yet it is not safe; and he who gains all that he can gain lawfully this year, possibly next year will be tempted to gain something unlawfully.

5. Let no man, for his own poverty, become more oppressing in his bargain; but quietly, modestly, diligently, and patiently recommend his estate to God, and follow its interest, and leave the success to him. For such courses will more probably advance his trade; they will certainly procure him a blessing and a recompense; and if they do not cure his poverty, they will take away the evil of it; and there is nothing else in it that can trouble him.

6. Do not detain the wages of the hireling; for every degree of detention of it beyond the time is injustice and lack of charity,

and grinds his face till tears and blood come out. But pay him exactly according to his covenant, or according to his needs.

7. Religiously keep all your promises and covenants, though made to your disadvantage, though afterward you perceive you might have done better. And let not any precedent act of yours be altered by any subsequent circumstance. Let nothing make you break your promise, unless it is unlawful or impossible.

8. Let no man appropriate to his own use what God, by a special mercy, or the republic has made common; for that is both against justice and charity too. And by miraculous accidents God has declared his displeasure against such enclosure. When the kings of Naples enclosed the gardens of Oenotria, where the best manna of Calabria descends, that no man might gather it without paying tribute, the manna ceased till the tribute was taken off, and then it came again. And so, after the third trial, when the princes found they could not have that in proper which God made to be common, they left it as free as God gave it. The like happened in Epire, when Lysimachus laid an impost upon the Tragasaean salt: it vanished, till Lysimachus left it public. And when the procurators of King Antigonus imposed a rate upon the sick people that came to Edepsum to drink the waters that were lately sprung, and were very healthy, instantly the waters dried up, and the hope of gain perished.

Section IV

Of Restitution

Restitution is that part of justice to which every man is obliged by a precedent contract, or a foregoing fault, by his own act, or another man's; either with or without his will. He who borrows is bound to pay, and much more he who steals or cheats. For if he who borrows and does not pay when he is able, is an unjust person and a robber, because he possesses another man's goods to the right owner's prejudice; then he who took them at first without leave, is the same thing, in every instant of his possession, in which the debtor is after the time in which he could have made payment. The act of stealing was soon over, and cannot be undone, and for it the sinner is only answerable to God, or his vicegerent; and he is in a particular manner appointed to expiate it by suffering punishment, and repenting, and asking pardon, and judging and condemning himself, doing acts of justice and charity, in opposition and contradiction to that evil action. But because, in the case of stealing, there is an injury done to our neighbor, and the evil still remains after the action is past; therefore for this we are accountable to our neighbor, and we are to take the evil off from him which we brought upon him, or else he is an injured person, a sufferer all the while. And that any man should be the worse on account of me, is against the rule of equity, of justice, and of charity: I do not do that to others which I would have done to myself; for I grow richer upon the ruins of his fortune.

Upon this ground, it is a determined rule in divinity, "Our sin can never be pardoned till we have restored what we have unjustly taken, or wrongfully detained"; restored it, I mean, actually, or in purpose or desire, which we must really perform when we can. And this doctrine, besides its apparent reasonableness, is derived from the express words of Scripture, reckoning restitution to be a necessary part of repentance, in order to the remission of our sins: "If the wicked restore the pledge, give again what he has robbed . . . he shall surely live, he shall not die" (Ezek. 33:15). The practice of this part of justice is to be directed by the following rules.

Rules of Making Restitution

1. Whosoever is a real cause of doing his neighbor wrong, by whatever instrument he does it (whether by commanding or encouraging it, by counseling or commending it, by acting or not hindering it when he might and ought, by concealing or receiving it), is bound to make restitution to his neighbor. Suppose you have persuaded an injury to be done to your neighbor which others would have persuaded if you had not; yet you are still obliged, because you did cause the injury, just

as they would have been obliged if they had done it; and you are not at all less bound by having persons as ill-inclined as you were.

2. He who commanded the injury to be done is first bound, then he who did it, and after these, they also are obliged who did assist, as without them the thing would not have been done. If satisfaction is made by any of the former, the latter is tied to repentance, but no restitution. But if the injured person is not righted, every one of them is wholly guilty of the injustice, and therefore bound to restitution singly and entirely.

3. Whosoever intends a little injury to his neighbor, and enacts it, and by it a greater evil accidentally comes, he is obliged to make an entire reparation of all the injury; of that which he intended, and of that which he intended not, but yet acted by his own instrument going farther than he at first proposed. He who set fire to a plane-tree to spite his neighbor, and the plane-tree set fire to his neighbor's house, is bound to pay for all the loss, because it did all arise from his own ill intention.

4. He who refuses to do any part of his duty (to which he is otherwise obliged), without a bribe, is bound to restore that money, because he took it in his neighbor's wrong.

5. He who by fact, word, or sign, either fraudulently or violently does hurt to his neighbor's body, life, goods, good name, friends, or soul is bound to make restitution in the several instances, according as they are capable of being made.

6. He who robs his neighbor of his goods, or detains anything violently or fraudulently, is bound not only to restore the principal, but all its fruits and wages which would have accrued to the right owner during the time of their being detained.

7. He who has wronged so many, or in that manner (as in the way of daily trade) that he knows not in what measure he has done it, or who they are, must redeem his faults by alms to the poor, according to the value of his wrongful dealing, as near as he can proportion it. Better it is to go begging to heaven, than to go to hell laden with the spoils of plunder and injustice.

Our duty to benefactors is to esteem and love their persons, to make them proportional returns of service, or duty, or profit, according to the greatness of their kindness, and to pray to God to make them recompense for all the good they have done us; which last office is also requisite to be done for our creditors, who in charity have relieved our wants.

PART II

THE RULE
AND EXERCISES
OF HOLY DYING

A General Preparation toward a Holy and Blessed Death, by Way of Consideration

Section I

Consideration of the Vanity and Shortness of Man's Life

A man is a bubble (said the Greek proverb), which Lucian represents with advantages, to this purpose, saying all the world is a storm, and men rise up in their several generations like bubbles descending from God and the dew of heaven, from a tear and drop of man, from nature and providence. And some of these instantly sink into the deluge of their first parent, and are hidden in a sheet of water, having had no other business in the world, but to be born, that they might be able to die. Others float up and down two or three turns, and suddenly disappear, and give their place to others. And they who live the longest upon the face of the waters are in perpetual motion, restless and uneasy, and being crushed with a great drop of a cloud, sink into flatness and a froth; the change not being great, it being hardly possible it should be more a nothing than it was before.

So is every man: he is born in vanity and sin; he comes into the world like morning mushrooms, soon thrusting up their heads into the air, and conversing with their kindred of the same production, and as soon they turn into dust and forgetfulness; some of them without any other interest in the affairs of the world, but that they made their parents a little glad, and very sorrowful. Others ride longer in the storm; it may be until seven years of vanity are expired, and then peradventure the sun shines hot upon their heads, and they fall into the shades below, into the darkness of the grave.

But if the bubble stands the shock of a bigger drop, and outlives the chances of a child, then the young man dances like a bubble, empty and gay, and shines like the image of a rainbow, which has no substance, and whose very imagery and colors are fantastical; and so he dances out of the gaiety of his youth, and is all the while in a storm, and endures, only because he is not knocked on the head by a drop of bigger rain, or crushed by the pressure of a load of indigested meat, or quenched by the disorder of an ill-placed humor. And to preserve a man alive in the midst of so many chances and hostilities, is as great a miracle as to create him; to preserve him from rushing into nothing, were equally the issues of an Almighty power.

Therefore the wise men of the world have contended who shall best fit man's condition with words, signifying his vanity and short abode. Homer calls a man a leaf, the smallest, the weakest piece of a short-lived, unsteady plant. Pindar calls him the dream of a shadow; another, the dream of the shadow of smoke. But St. James spoke by a more excellent spirit, saying, "Our life is but a vapor" (James 4:14), namely, drawn from the earth by a celestial influence, made of smoke, or the lighter parts of water; tossed with every wind, moved by the motion of a superior body; without virtue in itself, lifted up on high, or left below, according as it pleases the sun its foster-father.

But it is lighter yet. It is but appearing; a fantastic vapor, an apparition, nothing real. It is not so much as a mist, not the matter of a shower, or substantial enough to make a cloud. You cannot have a word that can signify a truer nothing. And yet the expression is made one degree more diminutive: a vapor, phantasm, or a mere appearance, and this but for a little while;

the very dream, the phantasm disappears in a small time, like the shadow that departs, or like a tale that is told, or as a dream when one awakes. A man is so vain, so unfixed, so perishing a creature that he cannot long last in the scene of fancy. A man goes off, and is forgotten like the dream of a distracted person. The sum of all is this: you are a man, than whom there is not in the world any greater instance of lights and shadows, of misery and folly, of laughter and tears, of groans and death.

And because this consideration is of great usefulness to many purposes of wisdom—all the succession of time, all the changes in nature, all the varieties of light and darkness, the thousand thousands of accidents in the world, and every contingency to every man—to every creature our funeral sermon does preach, and calls us to look and see how the old sexton Time throws up the earth, and digs a grave where we must lay our sins or our sorrows, and sow our bodies, till they rise again in a fair or in an intolerable eternity. Every revolution that the sun makes about the world, divides between life and death; and death possesses both those portions by the next day; and we are dead to all those months that we have already lived, and we shall never live them over again.

And still God makes little periods of our age. First we change our world, when we come from the womb to feel the warmth of the sun. Then we sleep and enter into the image of death, in which state we are unconcerned with all the changes of the world. And if our mothers or our nurses die, or a wild boar destroys our vineyards, or our king is sick, we regard it not; but during that state, we are as if our eyes were closed with the clay that weeps in the heart of the earth. At the end of seven years, our teeth fall and die before us, representing a formal prologue to the tragedy; and still every seven years it is odds but we shall finish the last scene. And when nature, or chance, or vice takes our body in pieces, weakening some parts and loosing others, we taste the grave and the solemnities of our own funerals, first in those parts that ministered to vice, and next in those that served for ornament; and in a short time even those that served necessity become useless, and entangled like the wheels of a broken clock. Baldness is but a dressing to our funerals, the proper ornament of mourning, and of a person entered very far into the regions of death. And we have many more of the same signification: grey hairs, rotten teeth, dim eyes, trembling joints, short breath, stiff limbs, wrinkled skin, short memory, decayed appetite. Every day's necessity calls for a reparation of that portion which death fed on all night, when we lay in his lap, and slept in his outer chambers. The very spirits of a man prey upon the daily portion of bread and flesh, and every meal is a rescue from one death, and lays up for another. And while we think a thought we die; and the clock strikes, and reckons on our portion of eternity. We form our words with the breath of our nostrils; we have the less to live upon for every word we speak.

Thus nature calls us to meditate on death by those things that are the instruments of acting it. And God, by all the variety of his providence, makes us see death everywhere, in all variety of circumstances, and dressed up for all the fancies and the expectation of every single person. Nature has given us one harvest every year, but death has two: the spring and autumn send throngs of men and women to graveyards; and all summer long men are recovering from their evils of the spring, till the dog days come, and then the Sirian star makes the summer deadly; and the fruits of autumn are laid up for all the year's provision, and the man who gathers them eats and indulges, and dies and needs them not, and he is laid up for eternity; and he who escapes till winter, only stays for another opportunity, which the distempers of that quarter minister to him with great variety. Thus death reigns in all the portions of our time. The autumn with its fruits provides disorders for us, and the winter's cold turns them into sharp diseases, and the spring brings flowers to strew our hearse, and the summer gives green turf and brambles to hind upon our graves. Fevers and excess, cold and chills, are the four quarters of the year, and all minister to death; and you can go nowhere but you tread upon a dead man's bones.

The wild fellow in Petronious, who escaped upon a broken table from the furies of a shipwreck, as he was sunning himself upon the rocky shore, espied a man rolling upon his floating bed of waves, ballasted with sand in the folds of his garment, and carried by his civil enemy the sea toward the shore to find a grave. And it cast him into some sad thoughts; that, peradventure, this man's wife, in some part of the continent, safe and warm, was looking for the good man's return next month; or, it might be, his son knew nothing of the tempest; or his father was thinking of that affectionate kiss which still was warm upon the good old man's cheek ever since he took a kind farewell, and he was weeping with joy to think how blessed he should be when his beloved boy returned into the circle of his father's arms. These are the thoughts of mortals; this is the end and sum of all their designs. A dark night and an ill guide, a boisterous sea and a broken cable, a hard rock and a rough wind dashed in pieces the fortune of a whole family; and they who shall weep loudest for the accident, are not yet entered into the storm, and yet have suffered shipwreck.

Then, looking upon the carcass, he knew it, and found it to be the master of the ship, who the day before cast up the accounts of his patrimony and his trade, and named the day when he thought to be at home. See how the man swims who was so angry two days since; his passions are becalmed with the storm, his accounts cast up, his cares at an end, his voyage done, and his gains are the strange events of death which, whether they be good or evil, the men who are alive seldom trouble themselves.

But seas alone do not break our vessels in pieces; everywhere we may be shipwrecked. A valiant general, when he is to reap the harvest of his crowns and triumphs, fights unsuccessfully, or falls into a fever with joy and wine, and changes his laurel into cypress, his triumphal chariot to a hearse; dying the night before he was appointed to perish in the drunkenness of his festival joys. It was a sad arrest of the feasts of the French court, when their king (Henry II) was killed really by the sportive image of a fight. And many brides have died under the hands of maidens dressing them for uneasy joys. Some have been paying their vows, and giving thanks for a prosperous return to their own houses, and the roof has descended upon their heads, and turned their loud religion into the deeper silence of a grave. And how many teeming-mothers have rejoiced over their swelling wombs, and pleased themselves in becoming the channels of blessing to a family; and the midwife has quickly bound their heads and feet, and carried them forth to burial? Or else the birthday of an heir has seen the coffin of the father brought into the house, and the divided mother has been forced to travail twice, with a painful birth, and a sadder death. There is no state, no occasion, no circumstance of our life, but it has been soured by some sad instance of a dying friend. A friendly meeting often ends in some sad mischance, and makes an eternal parting. And when the poet Eschylus was sitting under the walls of his house, an eagle hovering over his bald head mistook it for a stone, and let fall his oyster, hoping there to break the shell, but pierced the poor man's skull.

Death meets us everywhere, and is procured by every instrument, and in all chances, and enters in at many doors: by violence and secret influence; by the aspect of a star and the damp of a mist; by the emissions of a cloud, and the meeting of a vapor; by the fall of a chariot and the stumbling at a stone; by a full meal or an empty stomach; by watching at the wine or by watching at prayers; by the sun or the moon; by a heat or a cold; by sleepless nights or sleeping days; by water frozen into the hardness and sharpness of a dagger, or water thawed into the floods of a river; by a hair or a raisin; by violent motion or sitting still; by God's mercy or God's anger; by everything in providence, and everything in manners; by everything in nature and everything in chance. We take pains to heap up things useful to our life, and get our death in the purchase; and the person is snatched away, and the goods remain. And all this is the law and constitution of nature; it is a punishment to our sins, the unalterable event of providence, and the decree of heaven. The chains that confine us to this condition are strong as destiny, and immutable as the eternal laws of God.

I have conversed with some men who rejoiced in the death or calamity of others, and accounted it as a judgment upon them for being against them; but within the revolution of a few months, the same men met with a more uneasy and unpleasant death. When I saw this, I wept, and was afraid; for I knew that it must be so with all men; for we also shall die, and end our quarrels and contentions by passing to a final sentence.

Section II

The Consideration Reduced to Practice

It will be very material to our noblest purposes, if we represent this scene of change and sorrow a little more dressed up in circumstances, for so we shall be more apt to practice those rules, the doctrine of which is consequent to this consideration. It is a mighty change that is made by the death of every person, and it is visible to us who are alive. Reckon but from the sprightliness of youth, and the fair cheeks and full eyes of childhood; from the vigorousness and strong flexure of the joints of five and twenty; to the hollowness and dead paleness, the loathsomeness and horror of a three days burial, and we shall perceive the distance to be very great and very strange.

But so have I seen a rose newly springing from the clefts of its hood, and at first it was fair as the morning, and full with the dew of heaven, as a lamb's fleece; but when a ruder breath had forced open its virgin modesty, and dismantled its unripe retirements, it began to put on darkness, and decline to softness and the symptoms of a sickly age. It bowed the head, and broke its stalk, and at night, having lost some of its leaves and all its beauty, it fell into the portion of weeds. The same is the portion of every man and every woman; the heritage of worms and serpents, rottenness and cold dishonor, and our beauty so changed, that our acquaintance quickly knows us not; and that change is mingled with so much horror, that those who six hours ago tended upon us, either with charitable or ambitious services, cannot without some regret stay in the room alone where the body lies stripped of its life and honor.

I have read of a fair young German gentleman, who, living, often refused to be pictured, but put off the importunity of his friends' desire, by giving way that after a few days' burial they might send a painter to his vault, and, if they saw cause for it, draw the image of his death unto the life. They did so, and found his face half eaten, and his midriff and backbone full of serpents; and so he stands pictured among his armed ancestors. So does the fairest beauty change, and it will be as bad with you and me; and then, what servants shall we have to wait upon us in the grave? What friends to visit us? What officious people to cleanse away the moist and unwholesome cloud reflected upon our faces from the sides of the weeping vaults, which are the longest weepers for our funeral?

Rules and Considerations Regarding the Shortness of Life

This discourse will be useful, if we consider and practice the following rules and considerations:

1. All the rich and all the covetous men in the world will perceive, and all the world will perceive for them, that it is but an ill recompense for their cares, that by this time all that shall be left will be this, that the neighbors shall say he died a rich man. And yet his wealth will not profit him in the grave, but hugely swell the sad account. And he who kills the Lord's people with unjust or ambitious wars, shall have this character, that he threw away all the days of his life; that one year might be reckoned with his name, and computed by his reign or consulship. And many men, by great labors and affronts, many indignities and crimes, labor only for a pompous epitaph and a loud title upon their marble; while those, into whose possessions their heirs or kindred are entered, are forgotten, and lie as unregarded as their ashes, and without consequence or relation, as the turf upon the face of their graves.

A man may read a sermon, the best that ever man preached, if he shall but enter into the sepulchers of kings. Where our kings have been crowned, their ancestors lie interred, and they must walk over their forefather's head to take his crown. There is an acre sown with royal seed, the copy of the greatest change, from rich to naked, from ceiled roofs to arched coffins, from living like gods to die like men. There is enough to cool the flames of lust, to abate the heights of pride, to appease the itch of covetous desires, to sully and dash out the dissembling colors of a lustful, artificial, and imaginary beauty. There the warlike and the peaceful, the fortunate and the miserable, the beloved and the despised princes mingle their dust, and pay down their symbol of mortality, and tell all the world that, when we die, our ashes shall be equal to kings, and our accounts easier, and our pains for our crowns shall be less. To my apprehension it is a sad record which is left by Athenaeus concerning Ninus, the great Assyrian monarch, whose life and death is summed up in these words:

> *Ninus, the Assyrian, had an ocean of gold, and other riches more than the sand in the Caspian Sea. He was most valiant to eat and drink, and having mingled his wines, he threw the rest upon the stones. This man is dead: behold his sepulcher, and now hear where Ninus is. Sometime I was Ninus, and drew the breath of a living man, but now am nothing but clay. I have nothing but what I did eat, and what I served to myself in lust. That was and is all my portion. The wealth with which I was [esteemed] blessed, my enemies meeting together shall bear away. I am gone to hell; and when I went there, I neither carried gold, nor horse, nor silver chariot. I who wore a miter am now a little heap of dust.*

I know not anything that can better represent the evil condition of a wicked man. From the greatest secular dignity to dust and ashes his nature bears him; and from there to hell his sins carry him, and there he shall be forever under the dominion of chains and devils, wrath and an intolerable calamity. This is the reward of an unsanctified condition, and greatness ill gotten or ill administered.

2. Let no man extend his thoughts, or let his hopes wander toward far distant events. This day is mine and yours, but "we know not what we shall be tomorrow"; and every morning creeps out of a dark cloud, leaving behind it an ignorance and silence

deep as midnight, and undiscerned as are the phantoms that make a child smile. So we cannot discern what comes hereafter, unless we had a light from heaven brighter than the vision of an angel, even the spirit of prophecy. Without revelation we cannot tell whether we shall eat tomorrow, or whether an infection shall choke us. And it is written, in the unrevealed folds of divine predestination, that many who are this day alive shall tomorrow be laid upon the cold earth, and the women shall weep over their shroud, and dress them for their funeral. Whatever is disposed to happen, by the order of natural causes, or civil counsels, may be rescinded by a peculiar decree of providence, or be prevented by the death of the interested persons; who, while their hopes are full, and the work brought forward, and the sickle put into the harvest, even then if they put forth their hand to an event that stands but at the door, at that door their body may be carried forth to burial, before the expectation shall enter into fruition.

3. As our hopes must be confined, so must our designs. Let us not project long designs; the work of our soul is cut short, sweet, and plain, and fitted to the small portions of our shorter life. And as we must not trouble our inquiry, so neither must we intricate our labor and purposes, with what we shall never enjoy. This rule does not forbid us to plant orchards that shall feed our nephews with their fruit. For by such provisions we do charity to our relatives. But such projects are reproved as discompose our present duty by long and future designs; such as, by casting our labors to events at a distance, make us less remember our death standing at the door. It is fit for a man to work for his day's wages, or to contrive for the hire of a week, or to lay a train to make provisions for such a time as is within our eye, and in our duty, and within the usual periods of man's life; for whatsoever is necessary is also prudent. But while we plot and busy ourselves in the toils of an ambitious war, or the levies of a great estate; night enters in upon us, and tells the entire world how like fools we lived, and how miserably we died. Consider how imprudent a person he is who disposes of ten years to come, when he is not lord of tomorrow.

4. Though we must not look so far off, and pry abroad, yet we must be busy near at hand; we must, with all arts of the spirit, seize upon the present, because it passes from us while we speak, and because in it all our certainty consists. We must take our waters as out of a torrent and sudden shower, which will quickly cease dropping from above, and quickly cease running in our channels here below. This instant will never return again, and yet it may be this instant will declare or secure a whole eternity. The old Greeks and Romans taught us the prudence of this rule; but Christianity teaches us the religion of it. They so seized upon the present, that they would lose nothing of the day's pleasure: "Let us eat and drink, for tomorrow we shall die." That was their philosophy; and at their solemn feasts they would talk of death to heighten the present drinking, as knowing the drink that was poured upon their graves would be cold and without relish. Christianity turns this into religion. For he who by a present and a constant holiness secures the present, and makes it useful to his noblest purposes, turns his condition to his best advantage, by making his unavoidable fate become his necessary religion.

5. Since we stay not here, being people but of a day's abode, and our age is like that of a fly, and contemporary with a gourd; we must look somewhere else for an abiding city, a place in another country to fix our house in, whose walls and foundation is God, where we must find rest, or else be restless forever. For whatsoever ease we can have or fancy here is shortly to be changed into sadness or tediousness; it goes away too soon, like the periods of our life, or stays too long, like the sorrows of a sinner. Its own weariness, or a contrary disturbance, is its load; or it is eased by its revolution into vanity and forgetfulness. And where either there is sorrow or an end of joy, there can be no true felicity; which, because it must be had in some period of our duration, we must carry up our affections to the mansions prepared for us above, where eternity is the measure, felicity is the state, angels are the company, the Lamb is the light, and God is the portion and inheritance.

Section III

Rules and Spiritual Parts of Lengthening Our Days

1. In the accounts of a man's life we do not reckon that portion of days in which we were shut up in the prison of the womb; we tell our years from the day of our birth. And the same reason that makes our reckoning to stay so long, says also that then it begins too soon. For then we are indebted to others to make the account for us. For we know not of a long time, whether we are alive or not, having but some little approaches and symptoms of life. To feed, and sleep, and move a little—and imperfectly—is the state of an unborn child; and when he is born, he does no more for a good while. And what is it that shall make him be esteemed to live the life of a man? And when shall that account begin? For we should loathe having the accounts of our age taken by the measures of a beast. And fools and distracted persons are reckoned as civilly dead; they are no parts of the commonwealth, nor subject to laws, but secured by them in charity, and kept from violence as a man keeps his ox. And a third part of our life is spent before we enter into a higher order, into the state of a man.

2. Neither must we think that the life of a man begins when he can feed himself, or walk alone; when he can fight, or beget his own; for so he is contemporary with a camel or a cow. But he is first a man when he comes to a steady use of reason, according to his proportion; and when that is, all the world of men cannot tell precisely. Some are called at age at fourteen, some at twenty-one, some never; but all men late enough, for the life of a man comes upon him slowly and insensibly. But as when the sun approaches toward the gates of the morning, he first opens a little eye of heaven and sends away the spirits of darkness, and gives light to a woodcock, and calls up the lark to mattens; and by and by gilds the fringes of a cloud, and peeps over the eastern hills, thrusting out his golden horns, like those which decked the brow of Moses, when he was forced to wear a veil, because he had seen the face of God. And still while a man tells the story, the sun gets up higher, till he shows a fair

face and a full light, and then he shines one whole day, under a cloud often, and sometimes weeping great and little showers, and sets quickly.

So is a man's reason and his life. He first begins to perceive himself to see or taste, making little reflections upon his actions of sense, and can discourse of flies and dogs, shells and play, horses and liberty. But when he is strong enough to enter into arts, and little institutions, he is at first entertained with trifles and impertinent things, not because he needs them, but because his understanding is no larger; and little images of things are laid before him, like a cock-boat to a whale, only to play with it. But before a man comes to be wise, he is half dead with gouts and consumptions, with inflammations and aches, with sore eyes and a worn-out body. So that if we must not reckon the life of a man but by the accounts of his reason, it is long before his soul be dressed; and he is not to be called a man without a wise and an adorned soul, a soul at least furnished with what is necessary to his well-being. But by that time his soul is thus furnished, his body is decayed; and then you can hardly reckon him to be alive, when his body is possessed by so many degrees of death.

3. But there is yet another arrest. At first he lacks strength of body, and then he lacks the use of reason, and when that is come, it is ten to one but he stops by the impediments of vice, and lacks the strengths of the spirit. And now let us consider what that thing is which we call years of discretion. The young man has passed his tutors, and arrived at the bondage of a despicable spirit; he has run from discipline, and is let loose to passion. The man by this time has wit enough to choose his vice, to court his mistress, to talk confidently, ignorantly, and perpetually; to despise his betters, to deny nothing to his appetite, to do things of which when he is indeed a man he must forever be ashamed. For this is all the discretion that most men show in the first stage of their manhood: they can discern good from evil; and they prove their skill by leaving all that is good, and wallowing in the evils of folly and an unbridled appetite.

By this time the young man has contracted vicious habits, and is a beast in manners, and therefore it will not be fitting to reckon this the beginning of his life. He is a fool in his understanding, and that is a sad death; and he is dead in trespasses and sins, and that is a sadder. So he has no life but a natural one, the life of a beast or a tree; in all other capacities he is dead. He neither has the intellectual nor the spiritual life, neither the life of a man nor of a Christian; and this sad truth lasts too long. For old age seizes upon most men while they still retain the minds of boys, doing actions from principles of great folly and a mighty ignorance, admiring things useless and hurtful, and filling up all the dimensions of their abode with empty affairs, being at leisure to attend no virtue. They cannot pray, because they are busy, and because they are passionate. They cannot communicate, because they have quarrels and intrigues of perplexed causes; and therefore they cannot attend to the things of God; little considering that they must find a time to die in; that when death comes, they must be at leisure for that.

Such men are like sailors loosing from a port, and tossed immediately with a perpetual tempest, lasting till their cordage crack, and either they sink, or return back again to the same place. They did not make a voyage, though they were long at sea. The business and impertinent affairs of most men steal all their time, and they are restless in a foolish motion. But this is not the progress of a man; he is no further advanced in the course of life, though he reckon many years; for still his soul is childish, and trifling like an untaught boy.

Means of Lengthening Our Days

If the parts of this sad complaint find their remedy, we have by the same means cured the evils and the vanity of a short life. Therefore,

1. Be infinitely curious that you do not set back your life in the accounts of God by the intermingling criminal actions or contracting vicious habits. There are some vices that carry a sword in their hand, and cut a man off before his time. There is a sword of the Lord, and there is a sword of a man, and there is a

sword of the devil. Lust or rage, ambition or revenge, is a sword of Satan put into the hands of a man. These are the destroying angels; sin is the Apollyon, the destroyer that has gone out, not from the Lord but from the tempter; and we hug the poison, and twist willingly with the vipers, till they bring us into the regions of an irrecoverable sorrow.

We use to reckon persons as good as dead, if they have lost their limbs and their teeth, and are confined to a hospital, and converse with none but surgeons and physicians, mourners and divines, those dressers of bodies and souls for funeral. But it is worse when the soul, the principle of life, is employed wholly in the offices of death. And that man was worse than dead of whom Seneca tells, that being a rich fool, when he was lifted up from the baths, and set into a soft couch, asked his slaves, "Do I now sit?" The beast was so drowned in sensuality, and the death of his soul, that whether he did sit or not, he was to believe another. Idleness and every vice is as much of death as a long disease is, or the expense of ten years. "She who lives in pleasures is dead while she lives," says the apostle; and it is the style of the Spirit concerning wicked persons, "They are dead in trespasses and sins" (Eph. 2:1). For as every sensual pleasure, and every day of idleness and useless living, lops off a little branch from our short lives, so every deadly sin and every habitual vice quite destroys us; but innocence leaves us in our natural portions, and perfect period. We lose nothing of our life, if we lose nothing of our soul's health; and therefore he who would live a full age must avoid a sin, as he would decline the regions of death and the dishonors of the grave.

2. If we would have our life lengthened, let us begin with haste to live in the accounts of reason and religion, and then we shall have no reason to complain that our abode on earth is so short. Many men find it long enough, and indeed it is so to all senses. But when we spend in waste what God has given us in plenty, when we sacrifice our youth to folly, our manhood to lust and rage, our old age to covetousness and irreligion, not beginning to live till we are to die, designing that time to virtue, which indeed is infirm to everything and profitable to nothing,

then we make our lives short, and lust runs away with all the vigorous part of it, and pride and animosity steal the manly portion, and craftiness and interest possess old age; we spend as if we had too much time, and knew not what to do with it. We fear everything, like weak and silly mortals, and desire strangely and greedily, as if we were immortal. We complain our life is short, and yet we throw away much of it, and are weary of many of its parts. We complain the day is long, and the night is long, and we want company, and seek out arts to drive the time away, and then weep because it is gone too soon. Our life is too short to serve the ambition of a haughty prince, or a usurping rebel; our time too little to purchase great wealth, to satisfy the pride of a boastful fool, to trample upon all the enemies of our just or unjust interest.

Taking Account of Our Lives

But for the obtaining of virtue, for the actions of religion, God gives us time sufficient; if we make the outgoings of the morning and evening, that is, our infancy and old age, to be taken into the computations of a man; which we may see in the following particulars:

1. If our childhood, being first consecrated by a forward baptism, be seconded by a holy education and a complying obedience; if our youth be chaste and temperate, modest and industrious, proceeding through a prudent and sober manhood to a religious old age; then we have lived our whole duration, and shall never die, but be changed in a just time to a better and an immortal life.

2. If, besides the ordinary returns of our prayers, periodical and festival solemnities, and our seldom communions, we would allow to religion and the studies of wisdom those great shares that are trifled away upon vain sorrow, foolish mirth, troublesome ambition, busy covetousness, watchful lust, impertinent love affairs, and balls, reveling, and banquets, all that which was spent viciously and all that time that lay fallow and without employment, our life would quickly amount to a great sum. It is a vast work that any man may do, if he never should be idle. And

it is a huge way that a man may go in virtue, if he never should go out of his way. And he who perpetually reads good books, if his parts be answerable, will have a huge stock of knowledge. It is so in all things else. Strive not to forget your time, and suffer none of it to pass undiscerned; and then measure your life, and tell me how you find the measure of its continuance. However, the time we live is worth the money we pay for it; and therefore it is not to be thrown away.

3. When vicious men are dying, and seared with the alarming truths of an evil conscience, they would give the entire world for a year, for a month. Indeed, we read of some that called out with amazement, "Truce but till the morning"; and if a year, or some few months were given, those men think they could do miracles in it. And let us a while suppose what Dives would have done, if he had been loosed from the pains of hell, and permitted to live on earth one year. Would all the pleasures of the world have kept him one hour from the temple? Would he not perpetually have been under the hands of priests, or at the feet of the doctors, or by Moses' chair, or attending as near the altar as he could get, or relieving poor Lazarus, or praying to God, and crucifying all his sins?

I have read of a melancholic person who saw hell but in a dream or vision, and the amazement was such, that he would have chosen ten times to die rather than feel again so much horror; and it cannot be supposed but that such a person would spend a year in such holiness, that the religion of a few months would equal the devotion of many years. Let us but compute the proportions. If we should spend all our years of reason so as such a person would spend that one, can it be thought that life would be short and trifling in which we had performed such a religion, served God with so much holiness, mortified sin with such great labor, purchased virtue at such a rate and so rare an industry? It must be that such a man must die when he ought to die, and be like ripe and pleasant fruit falling from a fair tree, and gathered into baskets for the planter's use. He who has done all his business, and is born again to a glorious hope by the seed of a divine Spirit, can never die too soon, nor live too long.

Xerxes wept sadly when he saw his army of 2,300,000 men, because he considered that within a hundred years all that army would be dust and ashes. And yet, as Seneca well observes, he was the man who would bring them to their graves; and he consumed all that army in two years, for whom he feared after a hundred. Just so do we all. We complain that within thirty or forty years, a little more, or a great deal less, we shall descend again into the depths of our mother, and that our life is too short for any great employment; and yet we throw away thirty-five years of our forty, and the remaining five we divide between art and nature, civility and custom, necessity and convenience, prudent counsels and religion. But the portion of the last is little and contemptible, and yet that little is all that we can prudently account of our lives. We bring that fate and that death near us, of whose approach we are so sadly apprehensive.

4. In taking the accounts of your life, do not reckon by great distances, and by the periods of pleasure, or the satisfactions of your hopes, or the stating of your desires; but let every day and hour pass with observation. He who reckons he has lived but so many harvests, thinks they come not often enough, and that they go away too soon. Some lose the day with longing for the night, and the night in waiting for the day. Hope and fanciful expectations spend much of our lives; and, while with passion we look for a coronation, or the death of an enemy, or a day of joy, passing from fancy to possession without any intermediate notices; we throw away a precious year, and use it but as the burden of our time, fit to be pared off and thrown away; that we may come at those little pleasures which first steal our hearts, and then steal our lives.

5. A strict course of piety is the way to prolong our lives in the natural sense, and to add to the number of our years; and sin is sometimes by natural causality, very often by the anger of God, and the divine judgment, a cause of sudden and untimely death. Concerning which I shall add nothing but only the observation of Epiphanius, that for 3,332 years, there was not one example of a son who died before his father, but the course

of nature was kept—that he who was first born did first die (I speak of natural death, and therefore Abel cannot be opposed to this observation)—till Terah, the father of Abraham, taught the people a new religion, to make images of clay and worship them.* Concerning him it was first remarked that "Haran died before his father Terah in the land of his nativity" (Gen. 11:28). God, by an unheard-of judgment, punished his new-invented crime by the untimely death of his son.

6. But if I shall describe a living man, a man who has that life that distinguishes him from a fool or a bird, that which gives him a capacity next to angels; we shall find that even a good man lives not long, because it is long before he is born to this life, and longer yet before he has a man's growth. "He who can look upon death, and see its face with the same countenance with which he hears its story; who can endure all the labors of his life with his soul supporting his body; who can equally despise riches when he has them, and when he has them not; who does nothing for opinion sake, but everything for conscience, being as curious of his thoughts as of his acting in markets and theaters, and is as much in awe of himself as of a whole assembly; he who knows God looks on, and who contrives his secret affairs as in the presence of God and his holy angels; who loves his country, and obeys his prince, and desires and endeavors nothing more than that he may do honor to God"; this person may reckon his life to be the life of a man, because these are such things which fools and children, and birds and beasts cannot have; these are therefore the actions of life, because they are the seeds of immortality. That day in which we have done some excellent thing, we may as truly reckon to be added to our lives, as were the fifteen years to the days of Hezekiah.

---

*We learn from Joshua 24:2 that the progenitors of Abraham, and particularly Terah, served other gods in Ur of the Chaldees, but there appears to be no proof that he was the introducer of idolatry and image-worship in that country.

II

A General Preparation toward a Holy and Blessed Death, by Way of Exercise

Section I

Three Precepts Preparatory to a Holy Death,
to Be Practiced in Our Whole Life

1. He who would die well must always look for death, every day knocking at the gates of the grave, and then the gates of the grave shall never prevail upon him to do him mischief. This was the advice of all the wise and good men of the world, who especially in the days and periods of their joy, chose to throw some ashes into their chalices, some sober remembrances of their fatal period.

2. He who would die well, must all the days of his life lay up against the day of death; not only by the general provisions of holiness, but provisions proper to the necessities of that great day of expense, in which a man is to throw his last cast for an eternity of joys or sorrows; ever remembering, that this alone well-performed is not enough to pass us into paradise, but that this alone done foolishly is enough to send us to hell; and the

lack of either a holy life or death, makes a man to fall short of the mighty prize of his high calling.

In order to this rule, we are to consider what special graces we shall then need, and provide beforehand a reserve of strength and mercy. Men in the course of their lives walk lazily and incautiously; and when they are revolved to the time of their dissolution, they have no mercies in store, no patience, no faith, no love of God; being without appetite for the land of their inheritance, which Christ with so much pain and blood had purchased for them. When we come to die indeed, we shall be put to it to stand firm upon the two feet of a Christian: faith and patience. When we ourselves are to turn our former discourses into present practice, and to feel what we never felt before; then we shall find how much we have need to have secured the Spirit of God, and the grace of faith, by a habitual, perfect, immovable resolution. The same also is the case of patience.

It concerns us therefore highly in the whole course of our lives, not only to accustom ourselves to a patient suffering of injuries, affronts, persecutions, and losses; but also, by assiduous and fervent prayer to God all our life long, to call upon him to give us patience and great assistance, a strong faith and a confirmed hope, the Spirit of God and his holy angels assistants at that time, to resist and subdue the devil's temptations and assaults; and so to fortify our hearts, that they break not into intolerable sorrows and impatience, and end in wretchedness and infidelity. But this is to be the work of our lives, as God gives us time, by succession, by parts and little periods.

For it is very remarkable that God has scattered the firmament with stars, as a man sows corn in his fields. He has made a variety of creatures and gives us great choice of meats and drinks, although any one of both kinds would have served our needs, and so in all instances of nature. Yet, in the distribution of our time, God seems to be strait-handed, and gives it to us, not as nature gives us rivers, enough to drown us; but drop by drop, minute after minute, so that we never can have two minutes together, but he takes away one when he gives us another. This should teach us to value our time, since God so values it, and by his distribution of it, tells us it is the most precious thing we have. Since therefore in the day of our death we can still have but the same little portion of this precious time, let us in every minute of our life, prepare for our death.

3. He who desires to die happily, above all things must be careful that he does not live a soft, delicate, and voluptuous life; but a life severe, holy, and under the discipline of the cross; a life of warfare, labor, and watchfulness. No man lacks cause of tears and a daily sorrow. Let every man confess his sin, and chastise it; let him bear his cross patiently, and his persecutions nobly, and his repentances willingly and constantly; let him pity the evils of all the world, and bear his share of the calamities of his brother; let him long and sigh for the joys of heaven; let him tremble and fear because he has deserved the pains of hell. And by that time he has summed up all these labors and duties, all proper causes and acts of sorrow, he will find that for secular joy and wantonness of spirit, there are not left many void spaces in his life.

But besides this, a delicate life is hugely contrary to the hopes of a blessed eternity. "Woe to them who are at ease in Zion" (Amos 6:1); so it was said of old. And our blessed Lord said, "Woe to you who laugh, for you shall weep" (Luke 6:25); but, "Blessed are those who mourn, for they shall be comforted" (Matt. 5:4). Here or hereafter we must have our portion of sorrows. "He who now goes on his way weeping, and bears forth good seed with him, shall doubtless come again with joy, and bring his sheaves with him" (Ps. 126:6). And certainly he who sadly considers the portion of Dives, and remembers that the account which Abraham gave him for the inevitability of his torment was, because he had "his good things in this life," must in all reason, with trembling, run from a course of banquets, and "faring deliciously every day," as being a dangerous state, and a consignation to an evil greater than all danger, the pains and torments of unhappy souls.

Section II

Of Daily Examination of Our Actions in the Whole
Course of Our Health, Preparatory to Our Deathbed

He who will die well and happily must dress his soul by a
diligent and frequent scrutiny. He must understand and watch
the state of his soul; he must set his house in order before he is
fit to die. And for this there is great reason.

1. For if we consider the disorders of every day, the multitude of impertinent words, the time spent in vanity, the daily
omissions of duty, the coldness of our prayers, the indifference of our spirits in holy things, the uncertainty of our secret
purposes; our infinite deceptions and hypocrisies, sometimes
not known, very often not observed by ourselves; our lack of
charity, our not knowing in how many degrees of action and
purpose every virtue is to be exercised; the secret adherences
of pride, and too forward complacency in our best actions; our
failings in all our relations, our unsuspected sins in managing
a course of life certainly lawful, our little greediness in eating,
our too great freedom and fondness in lawful loves, our aptness
for things sensual, and our deadness and tediousness of spirit in
spiritual employments; besides an infinite variety of cases that
occur in the life of every man, and in all interactions of life; from
all this we shall find that the computations of a man's life are as
intricate as the accounts of eastern merchants; and therefore it
is reasonable that we should sum up our accounts at the foot of
every page, I mean, that we call ourselves to scrutiny every night
when we compose ourselves to the little images of death.

2. For, if we make but one general account, and never
reckon till we die, either we shall only reckon by great sums, and
remember nothing but clamorous and crying sins, and never
consider concerning particulars, or forget very many; or if we
could consider all that we ought, we must be confounded with
the multitude and variety.

3. It is not intended we should take accounts of our lives
only to be thought religious, but that we may see our evil and
amend it, that we may dash our sins against the stones, that we

may go to God, and to a spiritual guide, and search for remedies, and apply them. And indeed no man can well observe his
own growth in grace, but by accounting less frequent returns of
sin, and a more frequent victory over temptations; concerning
which, every man makes his observations according to how he
makes his inquiries and searches after himself.

4. And it will appear highly fitting, if we remember that
at the Day of Judgment not only the greatest lines of life, but
every branch and circumstance of every action, every word and
thought, shall be called to scrutiny; insomuch that it was a great
truth which one said, "Woe to the most innocent life, if God
should search into it without mixtures of mercy." And therefore
we are here to follow St. Paul's advice, "Judge yourselves, and
you shall not be judged of the Lord." The way to prevent God's
anger is to be angry with ourselves. As therefore every night
we must make our bed the memorial of our grave, so let our
evening thoughts be an image of the Day of Judgment.

Section III

General Considerations to Enforce the Former Practices

These are the general instruments of preparation, in order
to a holy death; it will concern us all to use them diligently and
speedily; for we must be long in doing that which must be done
but once. Therefore we must begin hastily, and lose no time;
especially since it is so great a venture, and upon it depends so
great a stake. Seneca said well, "There is no science or art in the
world so hard as to live and die well; the professors of other arts
are vulgar and many"; but he who knows how to do this business is certainly instructed to eternity.

Let me remember this; that a wise person will also put most
upon the greatest interest. Common prudence will teach us this.
No man will hire a general to cut wood, or shake hay with a
scepter, or spend his soul and all his faculties upon the purchase
of a cockleshell; but he will fit instruments to the dignity. Since
heaven is so glorious a state, and so certainly designed for us, let

us spend all that we have, all our passions and affections, all our study and industry, toward arriving there. For if we do arrive, every minute will infinitely pay for all the troubles of our whole life; if we do not, we shall have the reward of fools, a pitiless and an upbraiding misery.

To this purpose, I shall represent the state of lying and dead men in the devout words of some of the fathers of the church. When the sentence of death is decreed, and begins to be put in execution, it is sorrow enough to see or feel the sad accents of the agony and last contentions of the soul, and the reluctances of the body. The forehead washed with a new and stranger baptism, and smeared with a cold sweat, tenacious and clammy, apt to make it cleave to the roof of his coffin; the nose cold and undiscerning, not pleased with perfumes, nor suffering violence with a cloud of unwholesome smoke; the eyes dim as a sullied mirror, or the face of heaven, when God shows his anger in a storm; the feet cold, the hands stiff; the physicians despairing, our friends weeping, the rooms dressed with darkness and sorrow; and the exterior parts betraying the violences which the soul and spirit suffer. The nobler part, like the lord of the house, assaulted by exterior rudeness, and driven from all the out-works, at last faint and weary with short and frequent breathings, interrupted with the longer accents of sighs, without moisture, except the product of a spilt humor, when the pitcher is broken at the cistern, retires to its last fort, the heart, where it is pursued, and stormed, and beaten out, as when the barbarous Thracian sacked the glory of the Grecian empire.

Then calamity is great, and sorrow rules in all the capacities of man; then the mourners weep, because it is civil, or because they need you, or because they fear. But who suffers for you with a compassion sharp as is your pain? Then the noise is like the faint echo of a distant valley, and few hear, and they will not regard you, who seem like a person void of understanding, and of a departing interest. *Vere tremendum est mortis sacramentum* (Very awesome is the sacred act of death).

But these circumstances are common to all who die; and when a special providence shall distinguish them, they shall die with easy circumstances. But that which distinguishes them is this: he who has lived a wicked life, if his conscience be alarmed, and he does not die like a wolf or a tiger, without sense or remorse of all his wildness and his injury, his beastly nature led, if he had but sense of what he is going to suffer, or what he may expect to be his portion; then we may imagine the terror of the abused fancies of such, how they see alarming shapes, and because they fear them, they feel the gripes of devils, urging the unwilling souls from the embraces of their bodies, calling to the grave, and hasting to judgment, exhibiting great bills of uncancelled crimes, awakening and amazing their consciences, breaking all their hopes in pieces. Then "they look for some to have pity on them, but there is no man." No man dares be their pledge. "No man can redeem their souls," which now feel what they never feared. Then the trembling and the sorrow, memory of past sins, the fear of future pains, the sense of an angry God, and the presence of devils, consign them to the eternal company of all the damned and accursed spirits. Then they want an angel for their guide, and the Holy Spirit for their Comforter, and a good conscience for their testimony, and Christ for their Advocate, and they die and are left in prisons of earth or air, in secret and undiscerned regions, to weep and tremble, and infinitely to fear the coming of the day of Christ; at which time they shall be brought forth to change their condition into a worse, where they shall forever feel more than we can believe or understand.

But when a good man dies, one who has lived innocently, or made joy in heaven at his timely repentance, and in whose behalf the holy Jesus has interceded prosperously, and for whose interest "the Spirit makes intercessions with groans and sighs unutterable" (Rom. 8:26), and in whose defense the angels drive away the devils on his deathbed because his sins are pardoned, and because he resisted the devil in his lifetime, and fought successfully, and persevered unto the end; then the joys break forth through the clouds of sickness, and the conscience stands upright and confesses the glories of God. Then the sorrows of the sickness, and the flames of the fever, or the faintness of the consumption, do but untie the soul from its chain, and let it go forth, first into liberty, and then to glory. For it was but for a little while that the face of the sky was black, like the preparations of the night; but quickly the cloud was torn and rent, the violence of thunder parted it into little portions, that the sun might look forth with a watery eye, and then shine without a tear.

But it is an infinite refreshment to remember all the comforts of his prayers, the frequent victory over his temptations, the mortification of his lusts, the noblest sacrifice to God, in which he most delights, that we have given him our wills, and killed our appetites, for the interests of his services; then all the trouble of that is gone, and what remains is a portion in the inheritance of Jesus, of which he now talks no more as a thing at a distance, but is entering into the possession. When the veil is rent, and the prison doors are open, at the presence of God's angel, the soul goes forth full of hope, and instantly passes into the throngs of spirits, where angels meet it singing, and the devils flock with malicious and vile purposes, desiring to lead it away with them into their houses of sorrow. The soul passes forth and rejoices; passing by the devils in scorn and triumph, being securely carried into the bosom of the Lord, where they shall rest till their crowns are finished, and their mansions are prepared; and then they shall feast and sing, rejoice and worship forever and ever.

III.

Of the State of Sickness, and the Temptations Incident to It, with Their Proper Remedies

Introduction

Of the State of Sickness

If Adam had stood, he would not always have lived in this world; for this world was not a place capable of affording a dwelling to all those myriads of men and women which should have been born in all the generations of eternal ages, for so it must have been if man had not died at all. It is therefore certain man would have changed his abode: for so did Enoch, and so did Elijah, and so shall the entire world that shall be alive at the Day of Judgment. They shall not die, but they shall change their place and their abode, their duration and their state, and all this without death.

Section I

Of the First Temptation Proper to the State of Sickness: Impatience

Men who are in health are severe exactors of patience at the hands of those who are sick. It will be therefore necessary that we truly understand to what duties and actions the patience of a sick man ought to extend.

1. Sighs and groans, sorrow and prayers, humble complaints and dolorous expressions, are the sad accents of a sick man's language. For it is not to be expected that a sick man should act a part of patience with a countenance like an orator.

2. Therefore silence and not complaining are no parts of a sick man's duty, they are not necessary parts of patience. Abel's blood had a voice, and cried to God; and humility has a voice, and cries so loud to God that it pierces the clouds; and so has every sorrow and every sickness. And when a man cries out, and complains but according to his pain, it cannot be any part of a culpable impatience.

3. Some men's senses are so subtle, and their perceptions so quick that the same load is double upon them to what it is to another person. And therefore, comparing the expressions of the one with the silence of the other, a different judgment cannot be made concerning their patience.

4. Nature, in some cases, has made crying out to be an entertainment of the Spirit, and an abatement or diversion of the pain. For so did the old champions, when they threw their fatal nets that they might load their enemy with the snares and weights of death; they groaned aloud, and sent forth the anguish of their spirits into the eyes and heart of the man that stood against them. So it is in the endurance of some sharp pains, the complaints and shrieking, the sharp groans and the tender accents send forth the afflicted spirits, and force a way, that they may ease their oppression and their load; that when they have spent some of their sorrows by a burst forth, they may return better able to fortify the heart. Nothing of this is a certain sign, much less an action or part of impatience; and when our blessed Savior suffered his last and sharpest pang of sorrow, he cried out with a loud voice, and resolved to die, and did so.

Section II

Parts of Patience

1. That we may secure our patience, we must take care that our complaints be without despair. Despair sins against the reputation of God's goodness, and the efficacy of all our old experience. By despair we destroy the greatest comfort of our sorrows, and turn our sickness into the state of devils and perishing souls. No affliction is greater than despair; for that it is which makes hellfire, and turns a natural evil into an intolerable one; it hinders prayer, and fills up the intervals of sickness with a worse torture; it makes all spiritual arts useless, and the office of spiritual comforters and guides to be impertinent. Against this, hope is to be opposed. And its proper acts, as it relates to the exercise of patience, are a) praying to God for help, b) sending for the guides of souls, and c) using all holy exercises proper to that state which whoever does has not the impatience of despair.

2. Our complaints in sickness must be without murmur. Murmur sins against God's providence and government. By it we grow rude and, like the fallen angels, displeased at God's supremacy. Against this is opposed that part of patience, by which a man resigns himself into the hands of God, saying, with old Eli, "It is the Lord, let him do what he will" (1 Sam. 3:18); and, "Your will be done in earth, as it is in heaven" (Matt. 6:10). So the admiring of God's justice and wisdom does also fit the sick person for receiving God's mercy, and secures him the more in the grace of God.

3. Our complaints in sickness must be without peevishness. This sins against civility, and that necessary decency which must be used toward the ministers and assistants. By peevishness we increase our own sorrows, and are troublesome to them that stand there to ease ours. Against this are opposed easiness of persuasion and aptness to take counsel. The acts of this

part of patience are a) to obey our physicians, b) to not to be ungentle and uneasy to the ministers and nurses that attend us; but to take their kind offices as sweetly as we can, and to bear their indiscretions contentedly and without agitation within, or angry words without.

Section III

Remedies against Impatience, by Way of Exercise

1. The fittest means to enable us to esteem sickness tolerable is to remember that which indeed makes it so; and that is, that God does minister proper aids and supports to every one of his servants whom he visits with his rod. He knows our needs; he pities our sorrows; he relieves our miseries; he supports our weaknesses; he bids us ask for help, and he promises to give us all that; and he usually gives us more.

2. Prevent the violence and trouble of your spirit by an act of thanksgiving; for which, in the worst of sicknesses, you cannot lack cause, especially if you remember that this pain is not an eternal pain. Bless God for that; but take heed also lest you so order your affairs that you pass from hence to an eternal sorrow. If that is hard, this will be intolerable. But as for the present evil, a few days will end it.

3. Remember that you are a man and a Christian. As the covenant of nature has made it necessary, so the covenant of grace has made it to be chosen by you to be a suffering person. Either you must renounce your religion, or submit to God, and your portion of sufferings. And since our religion has made a covenant of sufferings, and the great business of our lives in sufferings, and most of the virtues of a Christian are passive graces, and all the promises of the gospel are passed upon us through Christ's cross; we have a necessity upon us to have an equal courage in all the variety of our sufferings. For without a universal fortitude, we can do nothing of our duty.

4. Never say, "I can do no more, I cannot endure this." For God would not have sent it if he had not known you strong enough to abide it; only he who knows you well already, would also take this occasion to make you know yourself. But it will be fit that you pray to God to give you a discerning spirit, that you may rightly distinguish just necessity from the flattery and fondness of flesh and blood.

5. Propound to your eyes and heart the example of the holy Jesus upon the cross. He endured more for you than you can, either for yourself or him. And remember, that if we are put to suffer, and do suffer in a good cause, or in a good manner; so that, in any sense, our sufferings are conformable to his sufferings; we shall reign together with him. The highway of the cross, which the King of sufferings has trodden before us, is the way to ease, to a kingdom.

6. The very suffering is a title to an excellent inheritance. For God chastens every son whom he receives, and if we are not chastised, we are bastards, and not sons. And be confident, that although God often sends pardon without correction, yet he never sends correction without pardon, unless it is your fault. And therefore take every or any affliction as an earnest of your pardon; and upon condition there may be peace with God, let anything be welcome that he can send as its instrument or condition. Suffer therefore God to choose his own circumstances of adopting you, and be content to be under discipline, when the reward of that is to become a son of God. And if this be the effect or the design of God's love to you, let it be the occasion of your love to him, and remember that the truth of love is hardly known unless something puts us to pain.

7. Use this as a punishment for your sins, and that God so intends it commonly is certain. If therefore you submit to it, you approve of the divine judgment. And no man can have cause to complain of anything but of himself, if either he believes God to be just, or himself to be a sinner; if he either thinks he has deserved hell, or that this little may be a means to prevent the greater, and bring him to heaven.

Section IV

Advantages of Sickness

1. I consider one of the great felicities of heaven consists in immunity from sin. Then we shall love God without mixture of malice, then we shall enjoy without envy; then we shall see fuller vessels running over with glory, and crowned with larger circles; and this we shall behold without spilling from our eyes (those vessels of joy and grief) any sign of anger, trouble, or a repining spirit. Our passions shall be pure, our love without fear, our possessions all our own; and all in the inheritance of Jesus, in the richest soil of God's eternal kingdom.

Now half of this reason that makes heaven so happy by being innocent, is also in the state of sickness, making the sorrows of old age smooth, and the groans of a sick heart fit to be joined to the music of angels. And though they sound harsh to our untuned ears and discomposed organs; yet those accents must be in themselves excellent which God loves to hear, and esteems them as prayers and arguments of pity, instruments of mercy and grace, and precursors to glory.

In sickness, the soul begins to dress herself for immortality. And first, she unties the strings of vanity that made her upper garment cleave to the world and sit uneasy. The flesh sits uneasy, and dwells in sorrow; and then the spirit feels itself at ease, freed from the petulant solicitations of those passions which in health were as busy and as restless as atoms in the sun.

2. Next to this, the soul, by the help of sickness, knocks off the fetters of pride and vainer complacencies. Then she draws the curtains, stops the light from coming in, and takes the pictures down—those fantastic images of self-love, and gay remembrances of vain opinion. Then the spirit stoops into the sobrieties of humble thoughts, and feels corruption chiding the forwardness of fancy, and allaying the vapors of conceit. She lays aside all her remembrances of applauses, all her ignorant confidences, and cares only to know Christ Jesus, and him crucified; to know him plainly, and with much heartiness and simplicity.

3. Next to these, as the soul is still undressing, she takes off the roughness of her anger and animosities, and receives the oil of mercies and forgiveness; fair interpretations and gentle answers, designs of reconciliation and Christian atonement. Wise men have said that anger sticks to a man's nature inseparably. But God, who has found out remedies for all diseases, has so ordered the circumstances of man that, in the worst sort of men, anger and great indignation consume and shrivel into little peevishness and uneasy accents of sickness; and in the better and more sanctified, it goes off in prayers, and alms, and solemn reconcilement.

4. Sickness is in some sense eligible, because it is the opportunity and the proper scene of exercising some virtues. It is that agony in which men are tried for a crown. And if we remember what glorious things are spoken of faith: that it is the life of just men, the restitution of the dead in trespasses and sins, the justification of a sinner, the support of the weak, the confidence of the strong, the warehouse of promises, and the title to very glorious rewards; we may easily imagine that it must have in it a work and a difficulty in some proportion answerable to so great effects.

But if you will try the excellency, and feel the work of faith; place yourself in a persecution, ride in a storm, let your bones be broken with sorrow, and your eyelids loosened with sickness; let your bread be dipped in tears, and all the daughters of music be brought low; then God tries your faith. Can you then trust his goodness, and believe him to be a Father, when you groan under his rod? Can you rely upon all the strange propositions of Scripture, and be content to perish if they are not true? Can you receive comfort in the discourses of death and heaven, of immortality and the resurrection, of the death of Christ, and conforming to his sufferings?

The truth is, there are but two great periods in which faith demonstrates itself to be a powerful and mighty grace: and they are the time of persecution and the approaches of death, for the passive part; and temptation for the active. In the days of pleasure, and the night of pain, faith is to fight, to contend for mastery. And faith overcomes all alluring temptations to sin, and all our weaknesses and fainting in our troubles. In our health and clearer days it is easy to talk of putting our trust in God; we readily trust in him for life when we have fair revenues, and for deliverance when we are newly escaped. But let us come to sit upon the margin of our grave, and let a tyrant lean hard upon our fortunes; let the storm arise, and the keels toss till the cordage crack—then can you believe, when you neither hear, nor see, nor feel anything but objections? This is the proper work of sickness. Faith is then brought into the theater, and so exercised, that if it abides but to the end of the contention, we may see that work of faith which God will hugely crown.

The same I say of hope, and of the love of God, and of patience, which is a grace produced from the mixtures of all these. They are virtues that are greedy of danger. God has crowned the memory of Job with a wreath of glory, because he sat upon his dunghill wisely and temperately; and his potsherd and groans, mingled with praises and justifications of God, pleased like an anthem sung by angels in the morning of the resurrection. God could not choose but be pleased with the accents of martyrs, when in their tortures they cried out nothing but "Holy Jesus," and "Blessed be God." And they also themselves, who, with a hearty resignation to the divine pleasure, can delight in God's severe dispensations, will have the transports of cherubim, when they enter into the joys of God.

Section V

The Second Temptation Proper to the State of Sickness: Fear of Death, with Its Remedies

There is nothing that can make sickness unsanctified but the same also will give us cause to fear death. If therefore we so order our affairs and spirits that we do not fear death, our sickness may easily become our advantage; and we can then receive counsel, and consider, and do those acts of virtue that are in that state the proper services of God.

Remedies against the Fear of Death, by Way of Consideration

1. God having in this world placed us in a sea, and troubled the sea with a continual storm, has appointed the church for a ship, and religion to be the stern. But there is no haven or port but death. Death is that harbor, to which God has designed every one, that there he may rest from the troubles of the world. Let us look on it as an act of mercy, to prevent many sins, and many calamities of a longer life and lay our heads down softly, and go to sleep without wrangling like disobedient children.

2. No good man was ever thought the more miserable for dying, but much the happier. When men saw the graves of Calatinus, of the Servilii, the Scipios, the Metelli, did ever any man amongst the wisest Romans think them unhappy? And when St. Paul fell under the sword of Nero, and St. Peter died upon the cross, and St. Stephen from an heap of stones was carried into an easier grave, they that made great lamentation over them wept for their own interest, and after the manner of men; but the martyrs were accounted happy, and their days kept solemnly, and their memories preserved in never-dying honors.

3. But when we consider death is not only better than a miserable life, but also that it is a state of advantage, we shall have reason not to double the sharpness of our sickness by our fear of death. To this all those arguments will minister which relate the advantages of the state of separation and resurrection.

Section VI

Remedies against the Fear of Death, by Way of Exercise

1. He who would willingly be fearless of death must learn to despise the world. He must neither love anything passionately, nor be proud of any circumstance of his life. "O death, how bitter is the remembrance of you to a man who lives at rest in his possessions, to a man who has nothing to vex him, and who has prosperity in all things."

2. He who would not fear death must strengthen his mind with Christian fortitude. The religion of a Christian does more command fortitude than ever did any institution; for we are commanded to be willing to die for Christ, to die for the brethren; to die rather than give offense or scandal. The effect of which is this: he who is thus instructed to do the necessary parts of his duty, is by the same instrument fortified against death. As he who does his duty needs not fear death, so neither shall he; the parts of his duty are parts of his security.

3. If God should say to us, "Cast yourself into the sea" (as Christ did to Peter, or as God concerning Jonas), "I have provided for you a dolphin, or a whale, or a port, a safety, or deliverance," would we not be incredulous and pusillanimous persons, if we should tremble to put ourselves into possession? The very duty of resignation and the love of our own interest, are good antidotes against fear. There is no reason, if we are pious, but that we should really desire death, and account it among the good things of God. St. Paul understood it well, when he desired to be dissolved; he well enough knew his own advantages, and pursued them accordingly. But it is certain that he who is afraid of death, either loves this world too much, or dares not trust God for the next.

IV.

OF THE PRACTICE OF THE GRACES PROPER TO THE STATE OF SICKNESS

Section I

Of the Practice of Patience

Now we imagine the man entering upon his scene of sorrows and passive graces. It may be he went yesterday to a wedding, merry and brisk, and there he felt his sentence, that he must return home and die; nor feared that then the angel was to strike his stroke till his knees kissed the earth, and his head trembled with the weight of the rod. But whatever the ingress was, when the man feels his blood boil, or his bones weary, or his flesh diseased; then he must consider that all those discourses he has heard concerning patience, and resignation, and conformity to Christ's sufferings, must now be reduced to practice; and pass from contemplation to such an exercise as will really try whether he was a true disciple of the cross. There would be no such thing as the grace of patience, if we were not to feel sickness; or enter into a state of sufferings where, when we are entered, we are to practice the following rules:

1. At the first address of sickness, stand still and arrest your spirit, that it may, without amazement or alarm, consider: this

was that which you looked for, and were always certain would happen, and that now you are to enter into the actions of a new religion. But at no hand suffer your spirits to be dispersed with fear, or wildness of thought; but stay their looseness and dispersion by a serious consideration of the present and future employment.

2. Do not choose the kind of sickness, or the manner of your death; but let it be what God shall please, so it is no greater than your spirit or your patience. And for that you are to rely upon the promise of God, and to secure yourself by prayer. But in all other things let God be your chooser, and let it be your work to submit indifferently, and attend your duty.

3. Be patient in the desires of religion, while you fear that by serving God less, you should run backward in the favor of God. Be content that the time that was formerly spent in prayer be now spent in vomiting, and carefulness, and attendances; since God has pleased it should be so, it does not become us to think hard thoughts concerning it. Do not think that God is only to be found in a great prayer, or a solemn office; he is moved by a sigh, by a groan, by an act of love. And therefore when your pain is great, lay all your strength upon it to bear it patiently. When the evil is something more tolerable, let your mind think some pious, though short, meditation; let it not be very busy, and full of attention, for that will be but a new temptation. If you can do more, do it; but if you cannot, let it not become a scruple to you. "If we cannot labor, yet let us love." Nothing can hinder us from that.

4. Let not the smart of your sickness make you call violently for death. You are not patient, unless you are content to live. God has wisely ordered it that we may be the better reconciled to death, because it is the period of many calamities. But wherever the general has placed you, stir not from your station until you are called off, but abide so, that death may come to you by the design of him who intends it to be your advantage. God has made patient endurance to be your work; and do not impatiently long for evening, lest at night you find the reward of him who was weary of his work.

Section II

Of the Practice of Faith in the Time of Sickness

Now is the time in which faith appears most necessary, and most difficult. It is the foundation of a good life, and the foundation of all our hopes. It is that without which we cannot live well, and without which we cannot die well. It is a grace that then we shall need to support our spirits, to sustain our hopes, to alleviate our sickness, to resist temptations, to prevent despair. The sick man may practice it in the following instances:

1. Let the sick man be careful that he does not admit of any doubt concerning that which he believed in his best health. Above all things in the world, let the sick man fear a proposition which his sickness has put into him, contrary to the discourses of health and a sober untroubled mind.

2. Let the sick man's faith especially be active about the promises of grace, and the excellent things of the gospel: things which can comfort him in his sorrows, and support his patience; those upon the hopes of which he did the duties of his life, and for which he is not unwilling to die; such as the intercession and the advocacy of Christ, remission of sins, the resurrection, the mysterious acts and mercies of man's redemption, Christ's triumph over death and all the powers of hell, the covenant of grace, or the blessed issues of repentance; and above all, the article of eternal life. This is the article that has made all the martyrs of Christ confident and glorious; and if it does not more than sufficiently strengthen our spirits to the present suffering, it is because we understand it not. But if the sick man fixes his thoughts here, he swells his hope, masters his fears, eases his sorrows, and overcomes his temptations.

3. Let the sick person be infinitely careful that his faith be not tempted by any man, or any thing; and when it is in any degree weakened, let him lay fast hold upon the conclusion, and by earnest prayer beg of God to guide him in certainty and safety. Consider that the article is better than all that is contrary or contradictory to it, and he is concerned that it is true, and concerned also that he does believe it. But he can receive no

good at all if Christ did not die, if there be no resurrection; if his creed has deceived him. Therefore all that he is to do is to secure his hold, which he can do in no way but by prayer and by his interest. And by this argument or instrument it was that Socrates refreshed the evil of his condition, when he was to drink his aconite: "If the soul be immortal, and perpetual rewards be laid up for wise souls, then I lose nothing by my death; but if there is not, then I lose nothing by my opinion, for it supports my spirit in my passage, and the evil of being deceived cannot overtake me when I have no being."

So it is with all who are tempted in their faith. If those articles are not true, then the men are nothing; if they are true, then they are happy. And if the articles fail, there can be no punishment for believing; but if they are true, my not believing destroys my entire portion in them, and the possibility to receive the excellent things that they contain. By faith we "quench the fiery darts of the devil" (Eph. 6:16); but if our faith be quenched, with what shall we be able to endure the assault? Therefore seize upon the article, and secure the great object and the great instrument; that is, the hope of eternal life through Jesus Christ.

Section III

Rules for the Practice of Repentance in Sickness

Let the sick man consider at what gate his sickness entered. If he can discover the particular, let him instantly, passionately, and with great contrition, dash the crime in pieces, lest he descend into his grave in the midst of a sin, and from there remove into an ocean of eternal sorrow. But if he only suffers the common fate of man, and knows not the particular inlet, he is to be governed by the following measures:

1. Supply the imperfections of your repentance with a general sorrow for the sins of your whole life: for all sins, known and unknown, repented and unrepented of; sins of ignorance or infirmity, which you know, or of which others have accused you;

your clamorous and your whispering sins; the sins of scandal, and the sins of a secret conscience, of the flesh and of the spirit.

2. To this purpose it is usually advised by spiritual persons that the sick man should make a universal confession, or a repetition of all the particular confessions and accusations of his whole life; that now at the foot of his account he may represent the sum total to God and his conscience.

3. Now is the time beyond which the sick man must on no account defer to make restitution of all his unjust possessions, or other men's rights, and satisfactions for all injuries and violences, according to his obligation and possibilities.

4. Let the sick person pour out many prayers of humiliation and contrition for all those sins which are spiritual, and in which no restitution or satisfaction can be made. For in some cases, penitential prayers are the only instances of repentance that can be made. If I have seduced a person who is dead or absent, and I cannot restore him to sober counsels by my discourse, and undeceiving him, I can only repent of that by way of prayer. And intemperance is no way to be rescinded or punished by a dying man but by hearty prayers.

Section IV

Of the Sick Man's Practice of Charity and Justice, by Way of Rule

1. Let the sick man set his house in order before he dies: state his cases of conscience, reconcile the fractures of his family, reunite brethren, cause right understandings and remove jealousies, give good counsels for the future conduct of their persons and estates, charm them into religion by the authority and advantages of a dying person; because the last words of a dying man are like the tooth of a wounded lion, making a deeper impression in the agony than in the most vigorous strength.

2. Let the sick man discover every secret which he is acquainted with, of art, or profit, physic, or advantage to mankind, if he may do it without the prejudice of a third person.

Some persons are so uncharitably envious, that they are willing that a secret receipt should die with them, and be buried in their grave, like treasure in the sepulcher of David.

3. Let him make his will with great justice and piety, that is, that the right heirs be not defrauded; and in those things where we have a liberty, that we take the opportunity of doing virtuously, that is, of considering how God may be best served by our donations, or how the interest of any virtue may be promoted; in which we are principally to regard the necessities of our nearest kindred and relatives, servants and friends.

4. It is proper for the state of sickness that we give alms in this state, so burying treasure in our graves that will not perish, but rise again in the resurrection of the just. Let the dispensation of our alms be as little entrusted to our executors as may be, except the lasting and successive portions; but with our own present care let us exercise the charity, and secure the stewardship.

5. In the intervals of sharper pains, when the sick man amasses together all the arguments of comfort, and testimonies of God's love to him and care of him, he must find infinite matter of thanksgiving; and it is a proper act of love to God, and justice too, that he gives honor to God on his deathbed for all the blessings of his life, not only in general communications, but also those by which he has been distinguished from others, or supported and blessed in his own person. So even Cyrus did upon the tops of the mountains, when by a fantasy he was warned of his approaching death:

Receive, [O God] my Father, these holy rites by which I put an end to many and great affairs; and I give you thanks for your celestial signs and prophetic notices, whereby you have signified to me what I ought to do, and what I ought not. I present also very great thanks that I have perceived and acknowledged your care of me, and have never exalted myself above my condition for any prosperous circumstance. And I pray that you will grant felicity to my wife, my children, and friends, and to me a death such as my life has been.

When these parts of religion are finished, according to each man's necessity, there is nothing remaining of personal duty to be done alone, but that the sick man act over these virtues by the renewing of devotion, and in the way of prayer; and that is to be continued as long as life, and voice, and reason dwell with us.

V.

OF VISITATION OF THE SICK

Section I

God, who has made no new covenant with dying persons, distinct from the covenant of the living, has also appointed no distinct sacraments for them, no other usages but such as are common to all the spiritual necessities of living and healthy persons. In all the days of our religion, from our baptism to the resignation of our soul, God has appointed his servants to minister to the necessities of souls, to bless, prudently to guide, and wisely to judge concerning them; and the Holy Spirit, that anointing from above, descends upon us in several effluxes, but ever by the ministries of the church. What the children of Israel begged of Moses, that God "would no more speak to them alone, but by his servant Moses," lest they should be consumed, God, in compliance with our infirmities, has of his own goodness established as a perpetual law in all ages of Christianity, that God will speak to us by his servants, and our solemn prayers shall be made to him by their advocation, and his blessings descend from heaven by their hands, and our offices return there by their presidencies, and our repentance shall be managed by them, and our pardon in many degrees ministered by them. God comforts us by their sermons, and reproves us by their discipline, and cuts off some by their severity, and reconciles others by their gentleness, and relieves us by their prayers, and instructs us by their discourses, and heals our sicknesses by their intercessions presented to God, and united to Christ's advocation. And in all this, they are no causes, but servants of the will of God, instruments of the divine grace, stewards and dispensers of the mysteries, and appointed to our souls to serve and lead, and to help in all dangers and necessities.

And they who received us in our baptism are also to carry us to our grave, and to take care that our end be as our life was, or should have been; and therefore it is established as an apostolic rule, "Is any man sick among you? Let him send for the elders of the church, and let them pray over him" (James 5:14).

Section II

Rules for the Visitations of Sick Persons

1. Let the minister be sent for, not only against the agony of death, but be advised within the whole conduct of the sickness; for in sickness indefinitely, and therefore in every sickness, and therefore in such which are not mortal, St. James gives the advice; and the sick man being bound to require them, is also tied to do it when he can know them, and his own necessity.

2. The interactions of the minister with the sick man have so much variety in them that they are not to be transacted at once; and therefore they do not well who send once to see the good man with sorrow, and hear him pray, and thank him, and dismiss him civilly, and desire to see his face no more. To dress a person for his funeral is not a work to be dispatched at one meeting. At one time he needs comfort, and another something to make him willing to die; and by and by he is tempted to impatience, and that needs a special cure; and it is a great work to make his confessions well and with advantages; and it may be the man is careless and indifferent, and then he needs to be made acquainted with the evil of his sin, and the danger of his person. And his cases of conscience may be so many and so

intricate, that he is not quickly to be reduced to peace; and one time the holy man must pray, and another time he must exhort, a third time administer the holy sacrament. And he who ought to watch all the periods and little portions of his life, lest he should be surprised and overcome, needs to be watched when he is sick, and assisted, and called upon, and reminded of the several parts of his duty, in every instant of his temptation.

3. When the ministers of religion have come, first let them do their ordinary offices; that is, pray for grace for the sick man, for patience, for resignation, for health (if it seems good to God in order to his great ends). For that is one of the ends of the advice of the apostle. And therefore the minister is to be sent for, not when the case is desperate, but before the sickness is come to its period. Let him discourse concerning the causes of sickness, and move him to consider concerning his condition. Let him call upon him to set his soul in order, to trim his lamp, to dress his soul; to renew acts of grace by way of prayer, to make amends in all the evils he has done; and to supply all the defects of duty, as much as his past condition requires, and his present can admit. When he has made this general entrance to the work of many days, he may descend to particulars by the following discourses.

Section III

Of Ministering in the Sick Man's Confession of Sins and Repentance

1. The first necessity that is to be served is that of repentance, in which the ministers can in no way serve him, but by first exhorting him to confession of his sins, and declaration of the state of his soul. For unless they know the manner of his life, and the degrees of his restitution, either they can do nothing at all, or nothing of advantage and certainty. His discourses, like Jonathan's arrows, may shoot short, or shoot over, but not wound where they should, nor open those humors that need a lancet or a cautery. To this purpose the sick man may be reminded that:

a. God has made a special promise to confession of sins. "He who confesses his sins and forsakes them shall have mercy" (Prov. 28:13); and, "If we confess our sins, God is righteous to forgive us our sins, and to cleanse us from all unrighteousness" (1 John 1:9).

b. Confession of sins is a proper act and introduction to repentance.

c. When the Jews, being warned by the sermons of the Baptist, repented of their sins, they confessed their sins to John.

d. The converts in the days of the apostles, returning to Christianity, instantly declared their faith and their repentance, by confession and declaration of their deeds, which they then renounced, abjured, and confessed to the apostles.

e. Without confession it cannot easily be judged concerning the sick person, whether his conscience ought to be troubled or not, and therefore it cannot be certain that it is not necessary.

f. There can be no reason against it but such as consults with flesh and blood, with infirmity and sin, to all which confession of sins is a direct enemy.

g. The ministers of the gospel are the "ministers of reconciliation," and are commanded "to restore such persons as are overtaken in a fault" (Gal. 6:1); and to that purpose they come to offer their ministry, if they may have cognizance of the fault and person.

h. In the matter of prudence, it is not safe to trust a man's self in the final condition of his soul; a man being no good judge in his own case and when a duty is so useful in all cases, so necessary in some, and encouraged by promises evangelical, by Scripture precedents, by the example of both testaments—he who for stubbornness, or sinful shamefacedness, or prejudice, or any other criminal weakness, shall decline to do it in the days of his danger, when the vanities of the world are worn off, and all affection to sin are wearied, this man, I say, is very near death, but very "far off from the kingdom of heaven" (Mark 12:34).

2. The spiritual man will find in the conduct of his duty, many cases and varieties of accidents that will alter his course and forms of proceedings. Most men are of a rude indifference, apt to excuse themselves, ignorant of their condition, abused by evil principles, content with a general confession. And if you provoke them to it by the foregoing considerations, lest their spirits should be a little uneasy, or not secured in their own opinions, will be apt to say, "They are sinners, as every man has his infirmity, and they as well as others; but, God be thanked, they bear no ill-will to any man, or are not adulterers, or rebels, or they fought on the right side, and God be merciful to them, for they are sinners." But you shall hardly open their breasts further, and to inquire beyond this would be to do the office of an accuser.

3. But, which is yet worse, there are very many persons who have been so used to a habitual course of a constant intemperance, or dissolution in any other instance, that the crime is made natural, and the conscience has digested all the trouble, and the man thinks himself in a good state. This happens in the cases of drunkenness and intemperate eating, idleness, mercilessness, lying, vain jesting, and particularly in spell evil which the laws do not punish, and public customs do not shame, but which are countenanced by potent sinners, or evil customs, or good nature, and mistaken civilities.

Instruments by Way of Consideration, to Awaken a Careless Person, and a Stupid Conscience

In these and the like cases the spiritual man must awaken the lethargy, and prick the conscience of the afflicted person, by representing to him that Christianity is a holy and a strict religion:

a. That many are called but few are chosen.
b. That the number of them who will be saved are but very few in respect of those who will descend into sorrow and everlasting darkness.

c. That we have covenanted with God in baptism to live a holy life.

d. That the measures of holiness in the Christian religion are not to be taken by the evil proportions of the multitude; because the multitude are those who do not enter into heaven, but the few, the elect, the holy servants of Jesus only.

e. That every habitual sin amounts to a very great guilt in the whole, though it be but in a small instance.

f. That if the righteous scarcely be saved, then there will be no place for the unrighteous and the sinner to appear in, but places of horror and amazement.

g. That confidence has destroyed many souls, and many have had a sad portion who have reckoned themselves saints.

h. That the promises of heaven are so great, that it is not reasonable to think that every man, and every kind of life, and an easy religion shall possess such infinite glories; that although heaven is a gift, yet there is a great severity and strict exacting of the conditions on our part to receive that gift.

i. That we are commanded to work out our salvation with fear and trembling; and that this precept was given with very great reason, considering the thousand thousands of ways of miscarrying.

j. That they who profess themselves servants of the institution, and servants of the law and discipline of Jesus, will find that they must judge themselves by the proportions of that law by which they were to rule themselves; that the laws of society and civility, and the voices of our company, are as ill judges as they are guides, but we are to stand or fall by his sentence who will not consider the talk of idle men, or the persuasion of willfully abused consciences; but of him who has felt our infirmity in all things but sin, and knows where our failings are unavoidable, and where and in what degree they are excusable; but never will endure a sin should seize upon any part of our love and deliberate choice.

k. That "if our conscience does not accuse, yet are we not hereby justified, for God is greater than our consciences"; that they who are most innocent have their consciences most tender and sensible; and that scrupulous persons are always most religious; and that to feel nothing is not a sign of life, but of death.

l. That nothing can be hid from the eyes of the Lord, to whom the day and the night, public and private words and thoughts, actions and designs, are equally discernible; that a lukewarm person is only secured in his own thoughts, but very unsafe in the event, and despised by God; that if he will cast up his accounts, even with a superficial eye, let him consider how few good works he has done, how inconsiderable is the relief which he gave to the poor, how little are the extraordinaries of his religion, and how inactive and lame, how polluted and disordered, were the ordinary parts and periods of it, and how many and great sins have stained his course of life; and until he enters into a particular scrutiny, let him only revolve in his mind what his general course has been, and in the way of prudence, let him say whether it was laudable and holy, or only indifferent and excusable; and if he can' think it only excusable, then he cannot but think it very fit that he should search into his own state, and take a guide, that he may make his access fairer when he shall be called before the dreadful tribunal of Christ in the clouds.

This is that which some spiritual persons call "awakening of the sinner by the terrors of the law"; but we have nothing to do with the terrors of the law; for, blessed be God, they concern us not. The terrors of the law were the curses upon all those who ever broke any of the least commandments, once, or in any instance; and to it the righteousness of faith is opposed. The terrors of the law admitted no repentance, no pardon, no abatement; and were so severe, that God never inflicted them at all according to the letter, because he admitted all to repentance who desired it with timely prayer, except in very few cases, as of Achan, Corah, or the like. But the state of threatening in the gospel is very fearful, because the conditions of avoiding them are easy, and they happen to evil persons after many warnings and frequent invitations to pardon and repentance. And in this sense it is necessary that such persons as we now deal with should be instructed concerning their danger.

4. When the sick man is either of himself, or by these considerations, set forward with purposes of repentance and confession of his sins in order to all its holy purposes, then the minister is to assist him in understanding the number of his sins, that is, the several kinds of them; for, as for the number of the particulars in every kind, he will need less help; and if he did, he can have it no where but in his own conscience, and from the witnesses of his conversation. Let this be done by prudent insinuation, by arts of remembrance, and secret notices, and propounding occasions and instruments of recalling such things to his mind, which either by public fame he is accused of, or by the temptations of his condition it is likely he might have contracted.

5. If the person is truly penitent, and forward to confess all things that are set before him or offered to his sight at a half face, then he may be complied with it in all his innocent circumstances, and his conscience be made placid and willing, and he may be drawn forward by kindness and civility, that his repentance in all the parts of it, and in every step of its progress, may be as voluntary and chosen as it can be. For by that means, if the sick person can be invited to do the work of religion, it enters by the door of his will, and will pass on toward consummation by the instrument of delight.

6. If the sick man is backward and without apprehension of the good-natured way, let the minister take care that by some way or other, the work of God be secured; and if he will not understand when he is secretly prompted, he must be asked in plain interrogatives concerning the crime of his

life. He must be told of the evil things that are spoken of him in markets and exchanges, the proper temptations and accustomed evils of his calling and condition, of the action of scandal. And in all those actions which were public, or of which any notice has come abroad, let care be taken that the right side of the case of conscience be turned toward him, and the error truly represented to him, by which he was abused, as the injustice of his contracts, his oppressive bargains, his plunder and violence; and if he has persuaded himself to think well of a scandalous action, let him be advised of his folly and danger.

7. And it concerns the minister of religion to follow this advice without partiality, or fear, or interest; in much simplicity, and prudence, and hearty sincerity; having no other consideration, than that the interest of the man's soul be preserved, and no caution used, but that the matter be represented with just circumstances, and civilities fitted to the person with prefaces of regard; so that nothing of the duty be diminished by it, that the introduction does not spoil the sermon, and both together ruin two souls, that of the speaker, and that of the hearer. For it may soon be considered, if the sick man is poor, yet his soul is equally dear to God, and was redeemed with the same price, and is therefore to be highly regarded. And there is no temptation, but that the spiritual man may speak freely without allaying interest, or fear, or mistaken civilities. But if the sick man is a prince, or a person of eminence or wealth, let it be remembered: it is an ill expression of reverence to his authority, or of regard to his person, to let him perish for the lack of an honest, and just, and free discourse.

8. Let the sick man in the scrutiny of his conscience and confession of his sins be carefully reminded to consider those sins which are only condemned in the court of conscience, and nowhere else. For there are certain secrecies, places of darkness and artificial veils, which the devil uses to hide our sins from us, and to incorporate them into our affections by a constant uninterrupted practice.

a. There are many sins that have reputation, and are accounted honor.
b. Others are permitted by law; as usury in all countries. And because every excess of it is a certain sin, the permission of so suspected a matter makes it ready for us.
c. Some things are not forbidden by human laws: as "lying in ordinary discourse, jeering, scoffing, intemperate eating, ingratitude, selling too dear, circumventing another in contracts, importunate entreaties, and temptation of persons to many instances of sin, pride, and ambition."
d. Some others do not reckon they sin against God, if the laws have seized upon the person; and many that are imprisoned for debt think themselves excused from payment; and when they pay the penalty, think they owe nothing for the scandal and disobedience.
e. Some sins are thought not considerable, but go under the title of sins of infirmity; such as idle thoughts, impatience, and anger.
f. Lastly, many things are thought not to be sins, such as misspending of time, whole days of useless and impertinent employment, winning men's money, censuring men's actions, curiosity, equivocating in the prices and secrets of buying and selling, rudeness, speaking truths enviously, and the like.

Under the dark shadow of these unhappy and fruitless yew trees, the enemy of mankind makes very many to be hid from themselves, sewing before their nakedness the fig leaves of impunity, public permission, a temporal penalty, infirmity, prejudice, and ignorance. Now in all these cases the ministers are to be inquisitive and observant, lest the fallacy prevail upon the penitent to evil purposes; and that those things which in his life passed without observation, may now be brought forth and "pass under saws and harrows"; that is, the severity and censure of sorrow and condemnation.

9. To which I add, for the likeness of the thing, that the matter of omission be considered; for in them lies the bigger half of our failings. And yet in many instances they are undiscerned, because they very often sit down by the conscience, but never upon it. And they are usually looked upon as poor men look upon their not having coaches and horses. It will be hard to make them understand their ignorance; it requires knowledge to perceive it, and therefore he who can perceive it, has it not.

10. The ministers of religion must take care that the sick man's confession be as minute and particular as it can be, and that as few sins as may be, be entrusted to the general prayer of pardon for all sins. For by being particular and enumerative of the variety of evils which disordered a man's life, his repentance is disposed to be more afflictive, and therefore more salutary; it has in it more sincerity, and makes a better judgment of the final condition of the man; and from there it is certain that the hopes of the sick man can be more confident and reasonable.

11. The spiritual man who assists at the repentance of the sick must not be inquisitive into all the circumstances of the particular sins, but be content with those that are direct parts of the crime, and aggravation of the sorrow such as frequency, long abode, and earnest choice in acting them; violent desires, great expense, scandal of others; dishonor to religion, days of devotion, religious solemnities, and holy places; and the degrees of boldness and impudence, perfect resolution, and the habit. If the sick person be reminded or inquired into concerning these, it may prove a good instrument to increase his contrition. But the other circumstances, as of the relative person in the participation of the crime, the measures or circumstances of the impure action, the name of the injured man or woman, the quality or accidental condition, these, and all the like, are but questions springing from curiosity, and producing scruple, and apt to turn into many inconveniences.

Section IV

Of the Ministering to the Reconciliation of the Sick Person

"If any man is overtaken in a fault, you who are spiritual restore such a one in the spirit of meekness" (Gal. 6:1), that is the commission, and, "Let the elders of the church pray over the sick man . . . and if he has committed sins they shall be forgiven him" (James 5:14–15), that is the effect of his power and his ministry. But concerning this, some few things are to be considered.

1. In all cases of receiving confessions of sick men, and assisting to the advancement of repentance, the minister is to apportion to every kind of sin such spiritual remedies as are apt to mortify the sin; such as abstinence from their occasions and opportunities, to avoid temptations, to resist their beginnings, restitution of wrongs, satisfaction of injuries, and acts of virtue contrary to the crimes. And although in great and dangerous sicknesses they are not directly to be imposed unless they are direct matters of duty, yet where they are medicinal they are to be insinuated, and in a general way remarked to him, concerning which when he returns to health, he is to receive particular advices.

2. The proper temptations of sick men for which a remedy is not yet provided, are unreasonable fears and unreasonable confidences, which the minister is to cure by the following considerations:

- a. "That Christ came into the world to save sinners" (1 Tim. 1:15).
- b. That God "delights not in the confusion and death of sinners" (Ezek. 18:32).
- c. That "in heaven there is great joy at the conversion of a sinner" (Luke 15:7).
- d. That Christ is a perpetual Advocate, daily interceding with his Father for our pardon.
- e. That God uses infinite arts, instruments, and devices to reconcile us to himself.

f. That he prays for us to be at peace with him and to be forgiven.

g. That he sends angels to keep us from violence and evil company, from temptations and surprises, and his Holy Spirit to guide us in holy ways, and his servants to warn and remind us perpetually. And therefore since certainly he is so desirous to save us, as appears by his Word, by his oaths, by his very nature, and his daily artifices of mercy, it is not likely that he will condemn us without great provocations of his majesty, and perseverance in them.

h. That the covenant of the gospel is a covenant of grace and of repentance, established with many great solemnities and miracles from heaven.

i. That although forgiveness of sins is consigned to us in baptism, and that this baptism is but once, and cannot be repeated; yet forgiveness of sins is the grace of the gospel, which is perpetually free for us.

j. That God in the old law, although he made a covenant of perfect obedience, and did not promise pardon at all after great sins; yet did give pardon, and declared it so to them for their own and for our sakes too. So he did to David, to Manasses, and to the whole nation of the Israelites ten times in the wilderness, even after their apostasies and idolatries. And in the prophets, the mercies of God and his remissions of sins were largely preached, though in the law God put on the robes of an angry Judge and a severe Lord. Therefore in the gospel, where he has established the whole sum of affairs upon faith and repentance, if God should not pardon great sinners who repent after baptism with a free dispensation, the gospel would be far harder than the intolerable covenant of the law.

k. It was concerning baptized Christians that St. John said, "If any man sins, we have an Advocate with the Father, and he is the propitiation for our sins" (1 John 2:1–2). And concerning lapsed Christians, St. Paul gave instruction, thus, "If any man be overtaken in a fault, you who are spiritual restore such a man in the spirit of meekness, considering lest you also be tempted" (Gal. 6:1). The Corinthian Christian committed incest, and was pardoned. And Simon Magus, after he was baptized, offered to commit his own sin of simony, and yet St. Peter bid him pray for pardon. And St. James says that if the sick man "sends for the elders of the church, and they pray over him, and he confess his sins, they shall be forgiven him" (James 5:14–15).

l. That God calls upon us to forgive our brother "seventy times seven times" (Matt. 18:22); and yet all that is but like the forgiving a hundred pence for his sake who forgives us ten thousand talents.

m. That if we can forgive a hundred thousand times, it is certain God will do so to us; our blessed Lord having commanded us to pray for pardon, as we pardon our offending brother.

n. That even in the case of very great sins, and great judgments inflicted upon the sinners, wise and good men have declared their sense to be, that God spent all his anger, and made it expire in that temporal misery; and so it was supposed to have been done in the case of Ananias. But that the hopes of any penitent man may not rely upon any uncertainty, we find in Holy Scripture that those Christians who had for their scandalous crimes deserved to be given over to Satan to be buffeted, yet had hopes to be saved in the day of the Lord.

o. That God glories in the titles of mercy and forgiveness, and will not have his appellatives so finite and limited as to expire in one act or in a seldom pardon.

But the minister must be infinitely careful that he does not go about to comfort vicious persons with the comforts belonging to God's elect, lest he prostitute holy things, and make them common, and his sermons deceitful, and vices be encouraged in others, and the man himself find that he was deceived, when he descends into his house of sorrow.

But because very few men are tempted with too great fears of failing, but very many are tempted by confidence and presumption, the ministers of religion had need be instructed with spiritual armor to resist this fiery dart of the devil.

Section V

Considerations against Presumption

I have already enumerated many particulars to provoke a drowsy conscience to a scrutiny and a suspicion of himself, that by seeing cause to suspect his condition, he might more freely accuse himself. But if either before, or in his repentance, he should grow too big in his spirit, so as that either he does violence to humility, or abates his care and zeal of his repentance, the spiritual man must allay his forwardness by representing to him:

1. That a man cannot think too meanly of himself, but very easily he may think too highly.

2. That a wise man will always, in a matter of great consequence, think the worst, and a good man will condemn himself with a hearty sentence.

3. That a man's heart is infinitely deceitful; unknown to itself, not certain in its own acts, praying one way, and desiring another, wandering and imperfect, loose and various, not understood of itself or anyone else, and deceitful beyond all the arts and numbers of observation.

4. That when we have done all that we can, we are unprofitable servants; and yet no man does all that he can do, and therefore is more to be despised and undervalued.

5. That the self-accusing publican was justified rather than the confident Pharisee.

6. That if Adam in paradise, and the angels in heaven, did fall, then it is prudent advice that we should not be highminded, but fear; and when we stand most confidently, take heed lest we fall. And yet there is nothing so likely to make us fall as pride and great opinions—which ruined the angels, which

God resists, which all men despise, and which betrays us into
carelessness, and a wretched, undiscerning, and unwary spirit.

Now the main parts of the ecclesiastical ministry are done,
and that which remains is that the minister pray over him, and
remind him to do good actions as he is capable: to call upon
God for pardon, to put his whole trust in him, to resign himself
to God's disposing, to be patient and even; to renounce every ill
word, or thought, or indecent action, which the violence of his
sickness may cause in him; to beg of God to give him his Holy
Spirit to guide him in his agony, and his holy angels to guard
him in his passage.

Section VI

Concerning the Treating of Our Departed Friends after Death, in Order to Their Burial

Solemn mourning is a good expression of our love to the
departed soul, and of his worth, and our value of him, and it
has its praise in public customs, but the praise of it is not in the
gospel; that is, it has no direct and proper uses in religion. For if
the dead died in the Lord, then there is joy to him; and it is an ill
expression of our affection and our charity to weep uncomfort-
ably at a change that has carried our friend to the state of a huge
felicity. But if the man did perish in his folly and his sins, there is
indeed cause to mourn, but no hopes of being comforted; for he
shall never return to light, or to hopes of restitution. Therefore
beware lest you also come into the same place of torment, and
let your grief sit down and rest upon your own turf, and weep
till a shower springs from your eyes to heal the wounds of your
spirit. Turn your sorrow into caution, your grief for him who is
dead to your care for yourself who are alive, lest you die and fall
like one of the fools, whose life is worse than death.

It is certainly a sad thing, to see a friend trembling with a
palsy, or scorched with fevers, or dried up like a potsherd with
immoderate heats, and rolling upon his uneasy bed without
sleep, which cannot be invited with music, or pleasant murmurs,

or a decent stillness. Nothing but the servants of cold death, poppy and weariness, can tempt the eyes to let their curtains down; and then they sleep only to taste of death, and make an essay of the shades below. And yet we weep not here. The opportunity for tears we choose when our friend is fallen asleep, when he has laid his neck upon the lap of his mother, and let his head down to be raised up to heaven.

When you have wept a while, compose the body to burial; which that it be done gravely, decently, and charitably, we have the example of all nations to engage us, and of all ages of the world to warrant. So that it is against common honesty, and public fame and reputation, not to do this office.

It is good that the body be kept veiled and secret, and not exposed to curious eyes, or the dishonors wrought by the changes of death, discerned and stared upon by impertinent persons. When Cyrus was dying, he called his sons and friends to take their leave, to touch his hand, to see him the last time; and gave a charge, that when he had put his veil over his face, no man should uncover it. Let it be interred after the manner of the country, and the laws of the place, and the dignity of the person.

Nothing of this concerns the dead; but it is the duty of the living. For to them it is all one whether they are carried forth upon a chariot or a wooden bier; whether they rot in the air, or in the earth; whether they are devoured by fishes or by worms. When Criton asked Socrates how he would be buried, he told him, "I think I shall escape from you, and that you cannot catch me, but so much of me as you can apprehend, use it as you see cause for, and bury it; but, however, do it according to the laws." Among Christians, the honor which is valued in behalf of the dead is that they be buried in places of religion, there where the field of God is sown with the seeds of the resurrection, that their bodies also may be among the Christians, with whom their hope and their portion is, and shall be forever.

Concerning doing honor to the dead, the consideration is not long. Anciently the friends of the dead used to make their funeral orations, and what they spoke of greater commendation was pardoned upon the accounts of friendship. But when Christianity seized upon the possession of the world, this charge was devolved upon priests and bishops, and they first kept the custom of the world, and adorned it with the piety of truth and of religion. But they also so ordered it that it should not be cheap, for they made funeral sermons only at the death of princes, or of such holy persons who shall judge the angels.

But that which is most considerable is that we should do something for the dead that is real and of advantage. That we perform their will, the laws oblige us, and will see to it; but that we do all those parts of personal duty which our dead left unperformed, and to which the laws do not oblige us, is an act of great charity. And it may redound to the advantage of our friends also, that their debts be paid even beyond the inventory of their belongings.

Besides this, let us right their causes and assert their honor. David added this also, that he did kindness to Mephibosheth for Jonathan's sake. And certainly it is the noblest thing in the world, to do an act of kindness to him whom we shall never see, but yet has deserved it of us, and to whom we would do it if he were present; and unless we do so, our charity is mercenary, and our friendships are direct merchandise. But what we do to the dead, or to the living for their sakes, is gratitude, and the noblest portion of humanity.

And yet I remember that the most excellent prince Cyrus, in his last exhortation to his sons upon his deathbed, charms them into peace and union of hearts and desires, by telling them that his soul would be still alive, and therefore fit to be revered and accounted as awful and venerable as when he was alive. And what we do to our dead friends is not done to persons undiscerning, as a fallen tree, but to such who better attend to their relatives, and to greater purposes, though in another manner than they did here below. It is ten to one but when we die we shall find the state of affairs wholly differing from all our opinions here, and that no man or sect has guessed anything at all of it as it is. Here I intend not to dispute, but to persuade. And therefore in the general, if it be probable that they know or feel the benefits done to them, though but by a reflex revelation from God, or some other communication from an angel, it may the rather incline us to our charities or duties to them respectively. However it be, it is certain they are not dead; and though we no more see the souls of our dead friends than we did when they were alive, yet we have reason to believe them to know more things and better.

And if our sleep be an image of death, we may also observe concerning it, that it is a state of life so separate from communications with the body, that it is one of the ways of oracle and prophecy by which the soul best declares her immortality, and the nobleness of her actions and powers, if she could get free from the body (as in the state of separation), or a clear dominion over it (as in the resurrection).

I have no other end in this discourse, but that we may be engaged to do our duty to our dead; lest peradventure they should perceive our neglect, and be witnesses of our transient affections and forgetfulness. Dead persons have religion passed upon them, and a solemn reverence. And if we think a ghost beholds us, it may be we have upon us the impressions likely to be made by love, and fear, and religion. However, we are sure that God sees us, and the world sees us. And if it is matter of duty toward our dead, God will exact it; if it is matter of kindness, the world will.

It remains, that we who are alive should so live, and attend the coming of the day of the Lord, that we may neither be surprised, nor leave our duties imperfect, nor our sins uncancelled, nor our persons unreconciled, nor God unappeased, but that when we descend to our graves we may rest in the bosom of the Lord, till the mansions be prepared, where we shall sing and feast eternally. Amen.

CPSIA information can be obtained
at www.ICGtesting.com
Printed in the USA
LVHW03s0208010918
588738LV00004B/6/P